Medical Instructions Towards the Prevention and Cure of Chronic Diseases Peculiar to Women

by John Leake

PRACTICAL OBSERVATIONS

ON THE

CHILD-BED FEVER,

AND THE

Acute Diseases

IN GENERAL, MOST FATAL TO

W O M E N

During the State of PREGNANCY.

By JOHN LEAKE, M. D.

Member of the Royal College of PHYSICIANS, London;
and Physician to the Westminster Lying-In Hospital.

FIFTH EDITION, with ADDITIONS.

V O L. II.

L O N D O N:

Printed for R. BALDWIN, in *Pater-Noster Row*; and
H. PAYNE, *Pall-Mall.*

M.DCC.LXXXI.

Monsieur Monsieur *John Leake*, docteur en medicine,
membre du collège royal des medicins de Londres, &c.

MAximâ cum voluptate et non sine fructû. Vir illustris-
sime, et ornatissime, tuum legi et relegi librum, cui
titulus est : *Practical Observations on the Child-Bed Fever*,
Printed London 1772. In illo enim reperi animadversio-
nes curiosas et plane novas de affectibus omenti, disquisi-
tiones nitidas, et sagaces, de curatione febris puerperium
insequentis, dubitationes quas dictarunt prudentia et
moderatio, contra systema nostri Celeberrimi *Levret*, co-
gitationes accuratas de hæmorrhagiis ante, et post partum.
Quid Magis ? in toto judicium et scientia veri bonique
medici refulget. his itaque perpensis, seu ægrorum salu-
tem, seu artis medicæ incrementum prospiciam, tuum
librum cunctis gratissimum duxi ; qua propter ut melius
innotescat, hunc in idioma gallicum converto, jam ferme
absoluta est interpretatio ; et paucos intra menses, si
tibi libet, prelo publico poterit in Franciâ committi.

Mihi familiaris et colendus amicus habet nunc sub
prelo tractatum idiomate Gallico scriptum de hæmorrhagiis uterinis. Plurimis abhinc mensibus auctori commu-
nicaveram versionem tuæ sectionis V.æ. *Of the nature*
and cause of uterine hæmorrhages, and their treatment, &c.
in hoc novo tractatu mei amici, multa sunt de te excerpta
cum laude tui ingenii et tui operis.

Auctor novi tractatûs, post expositionem variarum me-
thodorum contra hæmorrhagias uteri, nil efficacius inve-
niit quam obturatio vaginæ cum Linteolis vel siccis, vel
imbutis aceto, sed profunde immissis. Hæc methodus
olim vetustissimis nota, in oblivione quodam modo jace-
bat ; sed nunc resurgit longâ et felici experientiâ stabili-
ta ; et enim introductio linteorum in vaginâ, dum sistit
sanguinis fluxum, juvat quoque formationem coaguli ;
interim

interim uterus novas acquirit vires ; fefe conglomerat et conftringit, contractionibufque propellet coagulatum fanguinem et linteola immifla ; fed ut obturamentum vaginæ fit femper fauftum, plurimæ funt adhibendæ cautiones : fcilicet, mollis compreffio uteri cum manû, applicatio fupra pubem linteorum aquâ frigidâ, aut forfan melius aceto madidorum, ufus aeris frigidi, et, ut uno dicam verbo, quidquid poteft juvare uteri contractiones et vaforum fanguinem fundentium claufuram

Celeberrimus *Hoffman*, *Cornelius Trioen*, multique alii jam indicarant obturamentum vaginæ contra hæmorrhagias uteri ; hæc methodus tibi, Vir clariffime non erat ignota ; attamen in praxi vix erat explorata. In curriculo menfis proximi, ut opinor, novus tractatus mei amici evulgabitur ; et in illo videre poteris ferme omnia quæ fcripfifti de opio, medicamentis aftringentibus, venæ fectione, &c.

Vale, Vir clariffime ; et quanquam fim extraneus, et nullo modo tibi notus, non dedigneris, quæfo. meam finceram admirationem.

Datum Divione die 21. 7bris. 1775.

FRANCISCUS CHAUSSIER.

Chirurgiæ magifter in urbe Divionenfi apud Burgundos, acad. reg. chirurgiæ Parifienfis correfpondens, &c.

P. S. Si velis mihi refponfum dare. fubjungo infcriptionem epiftolæ in idiomate gallico.

A Monfieur Monfieur Chauffier. Maître en Chirurgie, &c, a Dyon.

Dr. Leake's PUBLIC LECTURES

ON

MIDWIFERY, and the *Difeafes peculiar to Women and Children*,

Will commence, from Time to Time, as ufual, at his THEATRE in Craven-Street, LONDON, where Particulars may be known.

GENERAL CONTENTS.

SEC-

CONTENTS.

SECTION IV.

SECTION V.

SECTION VI.

INTRODUCTION.

P. S. The Reader is requefted to correct fuch typographical Errors as have efcaped the Author's Attention, in this and the former Volume.

INTRODUCTION.

IF thofe Difeafes which have been found moft dangerous and mortal in their effects, ought principally to be confidered by phyficians ; none will more defervedly claim their attention than the *Child-bed Fever* ; as there is not, perhaps, any malady to which the human body is fubject, where powerful remedies of every kind have been tried with more diligence and lefs fuccefs. But, furely, this circumftance, difcouraging as it is, fhould

B   not

not render them regardless of the event, but rather increase their solicitude for the patient's safety, and induce them to try new methods of cure, since those hitherto adopted have so frequently failed.

Whilst I was preparing the following sheets for press, Dr. *Hulme* published a treatise on the same subject, the 29th of February 1772, where some points of doctrine being laid down as *new*, which I had repeatedly advanced, near three years before in my *public course of Lectures on Midwifery, and the Diseases incident to Women* ; I cannot, without injustice to myself on this occasion, omit the mention of the following circumstances, viz. That towards the end of the year 1769, and about the beginning of 1770, I attended several patients who laboured under the Child-bed Fever, both in private practice, and at the *Westminster Lying-in Hospital*, in consequence of being Physician to that charity.

As

As I gave *Lectures* on the *theory* and *practice* of *Midwifery*; I thought it my duty to communicate whatever I knew on that subject, to those gentlemen who did me the honor to attend as *pupils*; and therefore, in consequence of such observations as the daily occurrence of different cases, and frequent inspection of morbid bodies afforded me at the *Hospital* and elsewhere, I took the liberty to advance the following particulars. Namely, that the *omentum* was the part principally affected, having generally found it either almost totally consumed and melted down into a thick curd-like pus, or partially suppurated and inflamed; and that this inflammation had often overspread the surface of the intestines. A large quantity of purulent, whey-colored fluid was also found in the cavity of the abdomen and pelvis, mixed with small clots of blood and curd-like matter.

B 2

I also

I alſo laid it down, as my opinion, that this fever was not occaſioned by a tranſlation, or abſorption of *corrupted milk* from the breaſts, or any obſtruction of the *putrid lochia*; alſo, that it was not owing to an *inflammation* of the *uterus*, or to a morbid affection of that organ, as generally believed and aſſerted by different authors; and therefore, that it ought to be referred to other cauſes, as a *Diſeaſe of a peculiar nature*, and diſtinct from all others. However, the conformity between that gentleman's writings and mine may be ſolely confined to a deſcription of the characteriſtic ſymptoms of the diſeaſe, and its morbid appearances after death; in both which, as nature is generally uniform and conſiſtent with herſelf, any two authors tranſcribing from the ſame original muſt neceſſarily agree. But in what relates to the cauſes and cure of the diſeaſe; ſo far from ſimilarity of opinion, no doctrines can be found more oppoſite or diſſimilar.

At

At the same time I took occasion to mention an alteration of this article, in my *Syllabus of Lectures*, having, in a former impression (with *Hoffman*) called it the *Uterine Fever*, but being afterwards convinced there was nothing strictly uterine in that complaint; in the next impression, A. D. 1771, I gave it the name of Acute Fever peculiar to Women after delivery.

I also from experience recommended *early* and *copious bleeding*, with the antiphlogistic method, in preference to every thing else I had seen tried in the cure; and as a confirmation of these facts, I appeal to the gentlemen whose names are subjoined, at the conclusion, who attended and took notes of the several public courses of my Lectures, given in the three succeeding years 1770, 1771, and 1772; in which the several points of doctrine already mentioned, were circumstantially and repeatedly laid down.

Being not a little solicitous for the recovery of the patients intrusted to my care,

I spared no pains in giving my attendance by every possible opportunity, and also had the satisfaction of meeting Dr. *James Ford*, a gentleman deservedly eminent for his candor and skill, and one of the physicians of this hospital: But although we frequently consulted what was best to be done, and tried various medicines and methods for their relief, our best endeavors to that end often proved ineffectual.

It grieved me to find that so many women died of this destructive Fever, but since there was reason to believe it was at first imperfectly understood, I still had hopes that by time and observation, it might admit of more certainty in the cure, and become less formidable. I therefore, made it a rule to commit to paper the several symptoms and circumstances in the order they occurred, and also, the daily and hourly changes which happened at different periods of the disease; as far as opportunity would allow me, either from

my

my own attendance on the fick, or information of the *Matron*, or *Nurfes* in my
abfence. I noted down their degree of
violence and time of duration, as exactly
as poffible, and alfo, whether the patient
became better or worfe, in confequence of
fuch particular fymptoms as appeared from
time to time.

Thefe, the Reader may depend upon as
fo many *Facts*, or *clinical Minutes*, which
I collected as materials for a Hiftory of the
difeafe, and as for the deductions or practical inferences arifing from them, they
are fubmitted to the judgment and candor
of the medical reader, as matter of opinion, to be confirmed or corrected, as they
may be found to correfpond with obfervation and future experience.

The great variety of opinions prevailing among fpeculative men, in what relates to the origin and cure of difeafes, is
a convincing proof of the fallibility of the
human mind. The fubject of Phyfic is

attended

attended with so many difficulties, that we frequently deal in probable conjectures rather than certain truths; and this will always be the case in every science where so little can be decided by demonstration and actual experiment, and where the rest depends upon the caprice of our reasoning faculties, which are so insensibly perverted, and as it were led captive by the early prejudices of education, and reigning custom of countries; that things thus seen through different mediums, must necessarily strike our senses very differently, though in their own nature, they are uniformly the same.

Respecting the most powerful remedies, as *opium*, *mercury* and *bark*, such is the opposition of sentiments concerning their use, that one would almost be tempted to conclude, there was no true standard, no leading and unerring principles, by which to determine, either the effect of medicines, or the nature and event of diseases.

The

The division of diseases into *putrid* and *inflammatory*, however simple and neceffary it may appear, has been productive of much diffention and cavil among practitioners; but had they been lefs violent in contending about mere words, and more accurate in pointing out the true marks which conftitute the difference in thofe two claffes of difeafe, they would have deferved better of the profeffion, and the public.

With fome, almoft every diforder is fuppofed to be of the putrid kind; and therefore, Cordials, the Bark, and other antifeptics are directed as the fovereign remedies; and he that fhould venture to direct bleeding, would run the rifque of being called an executioner, rather than a phyfician. On the other hand, many in our own country, but efpecially in *France*, and the warmer climates, look upon moft Difeafes as inflammatory, and fuppofe, that nothing is fo requifite and effectual in
their

their cure, as Bleeding, Evacuations, and plentiful Dilution; and the methods recommended by the former, in the very fame fort of cafes, are deemed no better than rank poifons. Where Men are thus enflaved by cuftom, or actuated by blind zeal, they often err in violent extremes, and affert their opinions with as much confidence as if there was not even a poffibility of being miftaken; but, what is ftill worfe, they fometimes reflect on one another in terms the moft illiberal and unjuftifiable, to the difcredit of the Profeffion, and the injury of each other's reputation.

Which way are we to turn, where rocks lie on one fide, and quick-fands on the other?

Nothing has been fo great an obftacle to the improvement of fcience, as the partiality, and obfequious regard, which men have been apt pay great authorities; for whilft they difregard the teftimony of their own fenfes, and weakly or indolently

affent

affent to things as right, on the credit of others, they are feldom at much trouble to examine whether they are really fo or not; and errors early adopted, are either reluctantly corrected, or at laft, take fuch total poffeffion of the mind, that they become habitual, and are retained ever after.

Much refpect is certainly due to all fuch Authors as have fet down with candor and truth, whatever they knew in the cure of difeafes; but very often, inftead of plain facts, the Reader is prefented with fuch a medley of reality and fiction, partly from books; the Author's imagination, and the difeafe itfelf; that when he has perufed the whole, he is as much at a lofs as ever how to proceed in practice.

Of late, indeed, medical writers have happily withdrawn themfelves from the Fairy-land of hypothefis and conjecture; and, inftead of deviating from the folid path of nature, as many of them had for-

merly

merly done, are now principally guided by obſervation and practical experience.

Thoſe who mean to get uſeful knowledge, will therefore do well to take their information from the living body, by every opportunity of attending the ſick ; this will be going to the fountain-head, and reading, as it were, from the ample volume of Nature itſelf ; where the true ſtate of diſeaſe will more clearly unfold itſelf to the diligent obſerver ; the effects of medicine will be better known, and the methods of cure, from thence, become more certain and conſiſtent.

In the hiſtory of a diſeaſe, the ſeveral ſymptoms ought to be ſet down with ſimplicity and clearneſs, exactly as they preſent themſelves, without any innovation, conjecture, or falſe coloring ; which, having nothing to do with reality, would corrupt and adulterate the whole, and render it a mere recital of opinions and ſurmiſes, rather than a genuine deſcription of the diſ-

eaſe

eafe itfelf. A diftinction fhould alfo be made between fuch fymptoms as uniformly appear in the beginning, and are, as it were the immediate offspring of the difeafe; and thofe which are only occafioned by difference of conftitution, age, climate, or errors in diet: The firft ought to be confidered as the true and infeparable *pathognomonic figns*, which denote its nature and tendency, and from which the indication of cure is chiefly to be taken; the laft, only as accidental changes not fo much to be regarded.

The ftate of the air, together with the patient's age, and habit of body, fhould be mentioned; and the effect of medicines adminiftered at different times, whether good or bad, fhould alfo be faithfully and candidly fet down, and diftinguifhed from the fymptoms of difeafe, or the fimple efforts of nature; which, happily for the patient, are fometimes fuch as furmount every obftacle to a cure.

An

An accurate examination of the affected parts after death, by leading to the feat of difeafe, alfo tends to perfect its hiftory, and affift in throwing light on the cure; and this will always be moft neceffary in dangerous and uncommon cafes, where powerful medicines have been tried in vain. By attending to thofe morbid appearances, which have an intimate relation to fuch fymptoms as were imperfectly underftood, we proceed from effects to their caufes, which could never be done with fo much certainty by regarding the figns of the difeafe only. For inftance, it did not appear obvious from the fymptoms of *Child-bed Fever*, that the *omentum*, rather than the *uterus* or *inteftines*, was the part principally affected.

But although opening of bodies may afford much information, falfe inferences have often been made from them; for, all fuch *morbid appearances*, as there is reafon to believe did not exift till long after the

                                    invafion

invafion of the difeafe, ought to be looked upon as fo many confequences, and not the caufes of it.

The feat of difeafes is often apparent, tho' their caufes are frequently too remote for the difcovery of the moft acute and accurate obferver. But notwithftanding many changes are produced in the living body, for which no adequate or fatis-factory reafon can be affigned, there are fome certain appearances which almoft uniformly fucceed one another. For in-ftance, pain, from whatever caufe it may arife, if violent, will produce fpafm, fe-ver, or inflammation ; and thefe are often followed by fome critical evacuation, which is falutary ; or where that is wanting, by abfcefs or gangrene, which falling on the vital parts, will render the dif-eafe incurable. This has often been the cafe in the *Child-bed Fever*, and there-fore, fuch an unfavourable termination ought, if poffible, to be prevented by evacuations,

cuations, and the adminiſtration of medicines tending to carry off the morbid
cauſe by ſome of the natural ſecretions.

Sydenham has obſerved, that the fever
which follows a ſuppreſſion of *lochia*, ſometimes changed its type to that which prevailed in the epidemical ſeaſon.

That women after delivery, are more
diſpoſed to fever at one time than another, according to the conſtitution of the
air, cannot be doubted ; conſidering its
great influence on valetudinary habits,
and diſeaſes in general ; but particularly the *ſmall-pox, epidemical dyſentery,*
and *ulcerated ſore throat,* which not only
become more frequent, but alſo more
fatal, as the air changes from a healthy
to a malignant ſtate.

The great plague in *London,* A. D.
1636, which laſted twelve years, was more
or leſs fatal at different periods ; viz. in
eight years, one with another, two thou-

ſand

sand people died yearly, and never less than eight hundred in one year ; which shews that the contagion and its mortal effects, depended as much upon the state of air, as on the disease itself. This circumstance is still more clearly proved by the great disproportion of deaths in different weeks ; the number in one week increasing from one hundred and eighteen, to nine hundred and twenty-seven in the next ; and in another, decreasing from nine hundred and ninety-three, to two hundred and fifty-eight ; and from that number, again increasing, in the very next week, to eight hundred and fifty-two.*

How diseases are prodcued or influenced by the obvious qualities of air, is difficult to determine, notwithstanding all that has been said on the effects of heat and cold, moisture and dryness, or the winds blowing from particular quarters at certain seasons,

C

---

* Vide *Graut* on the Bills of Mortality.

fons, with different degrees of violence:
feeing, that very fudden changes of weather, from one extreme to another, frequently happen, without producing any
difeafes of the malignant or epidemic kind.
In like manner, a defect in the natural
fecretions, violent paffions of mind, or
errors in diet, at one time occafion fever and not at another; which evidently
fhew that the firft caufe of difeafes, whatever it is, acts more or lefs powerfully, as
the natural temperament of body concurs
to increafe or diminifh its effects.

In the year 1746, during the winter feafon, a difeafe of the epidemical kind was obferved to prevail with great violence among
lying-in women.* It began with a *diarrhœa*, followed by pains in the abdomen;
the *lochia* did not appear at their due time,
and the belly became hard, tenfe, and painful; the head was alfo affected with pain,

and

* Acad. des Sciences l'an. 1746, in 4to. Mem. p. 160.

and sometimes a cough attended : About the third or fourth day after delivery, the breasts which usually about that time were filled with milk, became flaccid, and about the fifth or seventh day the patient frequently died.

Poor women delivered in Hospitals, were observed most subject to this disease ; and in the month of *February* it became so extremely dangerous and epidemical, that scarcely one in twenty escaped it.

When the bodies of the deceased were opened, we are told, that *coagulum lactis* was found adhering to the exterior surface of the intestines, and *serum lacteum* contained in the abdomen. In some, the same kind of fluid was collected in the cavity of the breast. The *stomach*, *intestines* and *uterus*, had undergone inflammation ; and in many, the *ovaria* appeared diseased and suppurated.

The disease here mentioned seems to have been occasioned by a morbid affec-

tion

tion of the *uterus* ; and therefore, may be confidered as very different from that hereafter to be defcribed.

If the deaths of child-bed women depended upon the fame caufes as thofe which proved mortal in the fmall-pox, dyfentery, and reigning fevers of the feafon, as there was great reafon to fuppofe ; this circumftance could never have been fo truly known as by examining the *Bills of Mortality*, and remarking how far the deaths under the article *Child-bed* kept pace with thofe arifing from the above difeafes. But thefe bills are regulated with fo little care and exactnefs, either in refpect to the difeafes themfelves, or numbers faid to die of them ; that it would, from thence, be extremely difficult to determine this matter in a fatisfactory manner. The yearly bills would by no means be fufficient to do it ; becaufe although a greater than ufual number might die in the epidemic feafon ; in the fubfequent
months,

months, which make up the year, and which generally prove more healthy, the proportion of deaths might chance to be lefs; which, upon the whole, taking one year with another, would occafion but very little difference. I therefore regularly procured the weekly Bills of mortality, during the whole time of the *Child-bed Fever*, in order to afcertain this matter more exactly.

In the months of *January, February* and beginning of *March*, the difeafe prevailed with uncommon violence, and was evidently *epidemical* in different parts of the town; although on comparing the number of deaths occafioned by it, with thofe arifing from the *epidemics* of the feafon; I did not find that correfpondence which at firft I expected. However the great difference in the number of women who died in the year 1770, compared with that of the preceding year 1769, or the fubfequent year 1771, fufficiently and clearly proves

that

that this fever was epidemical in the firſt :
The number of deaths in the yearly bills
of mortality for the cities of *London* and
Weſtminſter, under this article, were as follows : From December the 13th, 1768, to
December the 12th, 1769, died in Child-
bed, *one hundred and eighty-five*. From
December the 12th, 1769, to December
the 11th, 1770, died, *two hundred and ſe-
venty* ; and from December the 11th, 1770,
to December the 10th, 1771, died, *one
hundred and ſeventy-two*. So that in the
year 1770, compared with the other two,
the number of deaths was very near a
third part more; and as this increaſe of
number did not happen uniformly, throughout the year, but was chiefly brought
about in that half of it, which commenced with December, and ended with May ;
it is ſtill more evident, that it could ariſe
from no other cauſe than a malignant conſtitution of the air.

But

But altho' it was proper and neceffary to mention the bills of mortality as a ftandard to which the reader might be referred; if I might be allowed to form a conjecture of the mortality of this difeafe, by what occurred to me, as well as feveral others of the profeffion, with whom I frequently converfed on the fubject; I fhould have no doubt, but, at leaft, half as many more women died of it, as thofe mentioned in the bills of mortality; which inftead of being fet down under the article *Child-bed Fever*, were indifcriminately placed to the account of *flux*, *pleurify*, or fome other diforder.

It is a public misfortune that thofe bills ftill continue to be kept in fuch a manner as to defeat their original intention, and to render all calculation in this matter vague and indeterminate.

Some years ago, an application was made to parliament by the company of parifh clerks, fetting forth the neceffity of

C 4

keeping

keeping an exact regifter of *births, burials,* and *marriages,* in all the parifhes throughout England; inftead of the prefent one including *chriftenings* and *burials* only, as confined to the parifhes within the bills of mortality for the cities of *London* and *Weftminfter.* Had this application been duly attended to, and fupported by parliament; many great and obvious advantages would have been the confequences of it ; for the healthy or unhealthy ftate of the air at particular times and places, might from thence have been more exactly afcertained ; as well as the increafe of population, in which the ftrength of every nation confifts.

HISTORY

HISTORY

OF THE

CHILD-BED FEVER.

SECTION I.

History of Child-bed Fever deduced from the Symptoms of that Disease, taken from the living Body, and an Examination of its morbid Appearances after Death.

AS it is evident that women, after delivery, are more subject to fevers during a distemperature of the air; I have, previous to the history of this disease, subjoined a short account of the weather, with a view to shew how far the symptoms might be increased or abated by its influence,

influence, during thofe months in which it was found moft *epidemical.*

Air is fo effential to the exiftence of all animals, that the want of it only for a few minutes is deftructive to life. It not only acts conftantly on the furface of their bodies by its preffure, but is alfo continually taken into the lungs by refpiration; and therefore, it is no wonder the health fhould be fo varioufly affected by it, as its qualities are changed and become more or lefs falutary. The difeafes which are *endemial* in particular countries, depend principally upon this circumftance; but human bodies being alfo affected by intemperance, and the paffions of the mind; thofe acute diftempers which fometimes rage, for a time, with uncommon violence, among brute animals living in the open fields, and in a ftate of nature, are more evident proofs of its powerful influence. The firft fhews that the atmofphere of particular places, is at all times more or lefs
                              unwholfome;

unwholfome ; the laft, that the atmofphere in general, may become fo for a
time, from variety of natural caufes which
notwithftanding are fo obfcure, that they
would fcarcely be known to exift, was it
not for their effects *.

A fhort account of the weather from
October 1769, to the end of May, 1770.

The month of October commenced with
fine clear weather, the wind in moderate
breezes being chiefly at N. N. E. From
the 5th to the 8th, it was bleak and cold,
with fome rain. From the 9th to the 13th,
the days were clear and frofty, with foggy
nights and mornings ; the wind being firft
wefterly, and afterwards fhifting from W.
to E. and then to E. N. E. From thence,
to the 25th, moift and mild weather, the
wind being variable ; a day or two of froft
then

---

* Here, it is only a tribute due to merit, to apprize the
reader of many curious and interefting difcoveries on the
properties of different kinds of *air*, lately publifhed by the
ingenious Dr. *Prieflley*.

then fucceeded, and the month ended with mifling rain and mild weather.

November began with mild weather, and fome fmart fhowers; till the 8th it was warm, moift and gloomy, the wind being chiefly at S. S. W ; the remainder of the month was extremely variable, the nights being frofty and the days fometimes clear and bright, and at other times overcaft with clouds, attended with mifling rain ; the wind fhifting to all points of the compafs, but chiefly to W. S. W.

December commenced with frofty clear days and foggy nights, the wind being variable; to the 8th, the weather in general was clear, but fometimes foggy with mifling rain, the wind being then chiefly at S. and E. S. E. with continual tranfitions from one extreme to another, viz. from a clear frofty air to cloudy damp weather with mifling rain ; and towards the end, froft with fleet and fnow ; the wind to the

2ad

22d being moſtly at W. and S. S. W. and afterwards it blowed from the N. to the N. N. W.

January began with moiſt weather, and a thick atmoſphere till the 4th, on which day there was a fall of ſnow, the wind being chiefly at W. N. W. and N. N. W to the 11th, ſmart froſty weather, with large quantities of ſnow, the wind at N. N. E. and N. N. W. From thence to the 17th, it was fair and rainy, bright and foggy by turns; on the 18th, a cold froſt began, with a large fall of ſnow, the wind at N. E; from thence to the 28th, mild, but variable, the wind being chiefly at S. or W. S. W. with moiſt gloomy weather, which concluded the month.

February began with fine weather, which continued to the 6th, the wind chiefly at S. W. from thence to the 8th, ſhowers of rain and ſnow, with a froſt, and the wind at N. To the 17th, changeable moiſt weather, the winds chiefly at S. or S. W.

On

On the 18th, alternate showers of hail, snow and rain ; from thence to the 22d, variable ; to the 25th, cold and bleak, with frost and some snow ; the wind being stationary at N. N. E ; to the end, the weather was cold, moist and cloudy, and the wind chiefly at S. W. and S.

March commenced with moist hazy weather, and a mild temperature of the air, with gleams of sun-shine, which continued to the 7th ; the wind continually shifting. To the 14th, it was cold and gloomy, with confiderable quantities of rain, the wind chiefly at N. E ; from thence to the 29th, sharp frost, with severe cold winds, and alternately, large falls of snow, and showers of fleet and hail ; the wind chiefly at E. N. E. This month ended with thaw and some rain, the wind then blowing from the south.

April began with rainy weather, and heavy showers of hail and fleet, the wind chiefly at W. and W. S. W ; from the 8th to the 14th, cold, bleak, wet weather, with more snow and hail, the wind being stationary at N. N. E; from thence to the 20th, fine weather, but showery; the wind at W. and W. S. W. This month concluded with severe wet weather.

May commenced with excessive cold rainy weather, and frequent showers of snow and hail, the wind at N. N. E. and N. N. W. From the 4th to the 8th, it changed to the S. and W. S. W. with cold heavy rains; from thence to the 16th, the weather in general was fine, with some thunder showers; to the 25th, cold, unsettled weather, and towards the end of the month, it was moist and hazy, the wind being at ~E. N. E.

Hippocrates observes, that a mild rainy winter succeeded by northerly winds in the spring, was dangerous to pregnant women*. Agreeable to this observation in the winter months, when the Child-bed

Fever

* De Aëre Locis et Aquis.

Fever began, the weather was obferved to be remarkably mild and moift, with a warmer temperature of air than was natural to the feafon ; and this was fucceeded by cold, bleak winds in the fpring, which were very unfriendly both to animals and vegetables.

About the 14th of March, 1770, a fharp froft commenced, with large falls of fnow, and alternate fhowers of fleet and hail, the wind being at North-eaft : This weather, which was uncommonly fevere, lafted till near the end of the month, at which time the malignant force of the Child-bed Fever feemed to abate; for altho' feveral women were affected with it at the *Hofpital*, foon after that time ; only two of them died, namely, *Ann Simms*, who was feized with it before the froft began, and *Ann Deufe*, who died the 29th of the fame month, juft at the commencement of thaw. The attack of the cold fit was lefs violent, and the fubfequent febrile fymptoms much more

more mild and favorable. The pulſe was neither ſo quick or weak, nor was the ſickneſs and vomiting ſo great; and inſtead of being followed as uſual, with pains in the bowels and griping bilious ſtools, the diarrhæa was moderate; the pulſe roſe in ſtrength, and a warm ſweat frequently broke out all over the body. Beſides, the ſecretion of milk was ſeldom interrupted, but continued plentiful; which, in general, may be looked upon as a favorable ſign; at leaſt, it ſhews that the violence of the diſeaſe, in ſuch caſes, is not ſo great as to take it away.

The Hiſtory of a diſeaſe will always be moſt perfect, where ſo little has been done by art, that the operations of nature remain free and undiſturbed. I ſhall therefore deſcribe this Acute Fever peculiar to women, after delivery, as it appeared when only aſſiſted by medicines of the ſimpleſt kind.

When the quickneſs of pulſe brought on by the efforts of labor does not afterwards

D ſoon

foon go off; it denotes fomething amifs in
the habit, tending to kindle up a fever,
which will always be found more dangerous, the fooner it invades the patient.

The *Child-bed Fever* generally commenced about the evening of the fecond, or beginning of the third day after delivery, with
a *rigor* or fhivering fit. Sometimes it came
on fooner, and though rarely, has been
known to appear as late as the fifth or
fixth day.

In many women, the attack was fudden,
without any apparent caufe or preceding
indifpofition; and foon followed by head-
ache, reftleffnefs, great ficknefs at ftomach,
and bilious vomitings.

Some had a bitter tafte in the mouth;
a naufea and univerfal langour; the countenance at firft was pale, and often much
altered, with a lifelefs, dim ftate of the
eyes, and an indolent pain over their orbits.
Thefe fymptoms would fometimes foretel
the approach of the difeafe, even before

any

any coldnefs or fhivering was perceived; but upon the whole, they may be confidered as *anomalous*, for in general, the fhivering preceded; and allowing for the difference of age and habit of body, there are perhaps few difeafes where the signs more regularly fucceeded each other, or where the morbid appearances after death, were found more exactly the fame.

Now and then, this Fever feemed to be brought on by *taking cold*, or *errors in diet*, but much oftener by *anxiety* of *mind*; and therefore, women of delicate conftitutions, very fufceptible and continually agitated by hopes and fears, are, of all others, the moft fubject to it, and recover with the greateft difficulty; confequently, unmarried women, for obvious reafons, were moft apt to be feized with it.

The degree of the cold fit was very different in different women; in fome, it would laft near an hour, and was fo intenfely violent as to fhake the body like

an

an ague; others were only affected with a
kind of thrilling fenfation, or temporary
chillnefs on the fkin, which foon went off
and returned by irregular periods.

When the fit lafted long and was violent,
I obferved great anxiety and oppreffion at
the breaft, attended with a laborious refpiration, but without pain; the patient was
often affected with deep fighing, and complained of great weight at the heart.

In thofe who were young and of a ftrong
habit, altho' the *rigor* was violent, its duration was fometimes fhort; and when the
pulfe rofe in ftrength and fulnefs, and became lefs frequent, it was fucceeded by a
better ftate of countenance, and the oppreffion was fooner removed from the *præcordia*; altho' no eruption appeared on the
breaft or body, as I at firft expected, till experience taught me otherwife.

In fuch cafes, which unfortunately occurred but feldom, an univerfal glow was
diffufed over the whole furface of body;
the

the skin began to be more florid, and a free perspiration came on with manifest relief, altho' it was not always lasting.

On the contrary; those who were slightly attacked in the beginning, often had a return of the febrile accession, and were alternately hot and cold throughout the day, especially if the pulse did not rise, but continued quick and weak. In such, the fever did not seem to run high; the tongue being very little altered from its natural state, nay, sometimes it was even moist and soft, and the thirst very inconsiderable; yet, in the end, they did not escape much better than others where it was more violent.

Those of lax fibres and of an irritable, hysterical habit, were oftenest thus affected; or where the constitution was much weakened by anxiety of mind, or a preceding bad state of health.

Sometimes the thirst was great, tho' the tongue had generally a better appearance

D 3

in

in the beginning than is common in other fevers, for it was feldom black or very foul; but as the difeafe advanced, became white and dry, with an increafe of thirft, and at laft was harfh and of a brownifh color towards the root, where it was coated with infpiffated, yellowifh mucus.

That perfpiration which proved falutary, overfpread the whole body, attended with moifture of the tongue and fauces, and alfo with abatement of thirft, ficknefs, and head-ache; but on the contrary, where the fweats were confined to the breaft, neck, and face, tho' they often continued to the laft, I never could obferve the leaft mitigation of the fymptoms; fuch partial fweats being the very effect of weaknefs and febrile anxiety, and not owing to any critical efforts of nature.

So great and fudden was the lofs of ftrength, that very few of the patients were able to turn in bed without affiftance, even fo early as the firft or fecond day after the attack;

attack; and moft of them continued helplefs throughout the whole progrefs of the
difeafe.

In the cold fit the pulfe was quick and
fmall, and the pulfations fo feeble and indiftinct, that fometimes I was hardly able
to number them exactly. When the hot
fit came on, tho' it was then more full and
diftinct, it ftill remained quick, but was
feldom hard or ftrong, except in few inftances, where the patient was young and
plethoric. In general, it would beat from
ninety to *one hundred* and *thirty-feven* ftrokes
in a minute; varying by turns in ftrength
and frequency from the loweft to the high-
eft of thefe numbers, and *vice verfa*, in
proportion to the ftrength or weaknefs of
the habit, and violence of the attack. An
excefs or defect of the natural fecretions,
the ftate of mind, with many other accidental caufes, will be found to produce
great alteration in the pulfe, both in refpect
to its ftrength and quicknefs.

The

The sympathy between the head and stomach is so great, that it is sometimes difficult to distinguish which of them is first affected; but in this disease, the head-ache generally preceded the sickness at stomach; where the last was great, the patient vomited spontaneously; otherwise, the nausea continued till a purging began, and then usually ceased. The last was always most violent when nothing had previously been rejected by vomit.

It is here necessary, to distinguish this febrile head-ache, from that which very commonly happens at the coming of milk, when the body is costive; the first may be relieved by a gentle emetic, the last may be effectually taken away by cathartic clysters and laxatives.

The first attack of this fever is sometimes so violent, that in many respects, it resembles the *cholera morbus*; for the pain, sickness, and burning heat in the stomach ftomach and bowels, are almoft the fame ; and the bile, in great profufion, is difcharged upwards and downwards ; tho' in the firft, the pulfe is more quick and weak.

The fluid rejected by the ftomach was yellow and ropy, and feemed to be a mixture of bile with large quantities of gaftric mucus; fometimes it was green and porraceous, but when the vomiting continued till the advanced ftate of the difeafe, or returned towards the end ; it was then watery and of a *blackifh color.*

The ficknefs at ftomach was always much relieved by vomiting ; but when that abated, a violent purging came on, with fevere gripings and pain in the bowels.

The vomiting attending this fever, fhould always be diftinguifhed from that which often accompanies a quick labor from the violent efforts of the uterus ; the laft is not bilious, and foon goes off after delivery,

delivery, without any bad confequence or fubfequent fever.

At the beginning of the diarrhæa, the ftools were yellow, frothy, and mixed with mucus; fometimes they were greenifh, but towards the end of the dif-eafe, at which time they often became in-voluntary, they were blackifh, fœtid, and more dilute, refembling the color of *mofs water.*

I never faw this fever appear with any degree of violence, but it was always at-tended with an obftinate diarrhæa; many of the patients had eight or ten evacua-tions in fix or eight hours, which were followed by fhort intervals of eafe; but neither the quicknefs of pulfe, thirft, nor any of the febrile fymptoms were in the leaft abated by the difcharge, altho' it was fo frequent and profufe.

In fhort, the diarrhæa was evidently *fymptomatic,* and only procured a refpite from pain by evacuating the offending bile:

bile: It depended so very much upon the fever, that whenever it obstinately continued, the diarrhæa remained unconquerable; and even altho' that seemed to abate for a time, as in the case of *Juliana Thompson*, it often came on again with violence, and so continued till the patient's death, whenever there was a return of the febrile accession.

Here, the diarrhæa seemed plainly to arise from the effect of fever, which increases the irritability of all the abdominal viscera, and renders them more liable to pain and inflammation. The immoderate secretion of bile, was also manifestly the effect, and not the cause of fever; which from its acrimony and redundance increased the purging, by stimulating the intestines to expel their contents. On the contrary, when the pulse abated in frequency, and the inflammatory symptoms subsided; the purging was proportionally less, and even when it continued longer than

than ufual, it was not then attended with the fame lofs of ftrength, but appeared fimply colliquative.

About the fecond day after the cold fit, the patient complained much of pain at the pit of her ftomach, darting down towards the navel, and fometimes from thence to the fhort ribs and fides: Now and then, as the difeafe advanced, fome had acute pain under the fhoulder-blade, which ftruck obliquely downwards and forwards, from the thorax to the ftomach; thefe pains were always moft violent and intolerable during infpiration, which became interrupted and defultory, or in thefe other words, they breathed with difficulty and as it were by jirks. Some had a cough, which generally was moft troublefome in the decline of the difeafe.

In feveral, the belly began to fwell about the third or fourth day, from the commencement of the fever, and became extremely tenfe and prominent, as in the cafe

of

of *Juliana Thompson* and *Margaret Walker*, both of whom died. Whenever this swelling came on whilst the purging continued, and especially if it closely followed the pain, extending from the stomach to the navel; as far as I had an opportunity to observe, it was always a *mortal sign*; for not one of them recovered who were thus affected.

This morbid enlargement and tension of the abdomen supervening the pain at the umbilical region, should however be distinguished from the accidental swelling of the belly from the confinement of air in the intestines, which sometimes happens by a sudden cessation of the purging; and which will soon go off without danger by the use of laxative medicines.

About this period of the disease, the patient had a wild, distressed, eager countenance, and a trembling hand; a local *crimson color* appeared in her cheeks; her lips were of a *livid hue*, and her nostrils

tense

tenfe and expanded. When thefe fymptoms prevailed with violence, neither art
nor nature were fufficient to procure relief.

*The Lochia from firft to laft, were not ob-
ftructed nor deficient in quantity,* neither
did the quality of this difcharge feem to
be in the leaft altered from its natural
ftate ; a prefumption that the *uterus* was
not at all affected. Of this circumftance
I was convinced, by making confiderable
preffure above the *pubes* with my hand,
which did not occafion pain ; but when
the fame degree of preffure was applied
higher, between the ftomach and umbilical region, it became intolerable.

Hence it appears, that the *uterus is not
originally affected,* fo as to produce this
fever, neither does it ufually fuffer by fympathy, in proportion with the other parts,
as will be more evidently fhewn hereafter.

*The fecretion of Milk was generally inter-
rupted* by the attack of the cold fit, and
fometimes

sometimes it was almost taken away; at other times it continued in a moderate degree for several days after, even 'till within a short time of the patient's death.

A slight chillness usually precedes the coming of milk, which is often mistaken for that morbid shivering with which this fever commences; but with a little care, it will not be difficult to distinguish the one from the other; for, the first happens before the milk is collected, and is usually followed by a plentiful flow of it; but the last, generally comes on after a secretion of that fluid is begun, which not unfrequently afterwards carries it off. From mistakes of this kind, I have sometimes been called in where there was no occasion; for when the disease was rife, and many died, the least appearance of it was very alarming to child-bed women, and those about them. Indeed, when a slight degree of this morbid shivering comes on exactly at the time of the milk-

fever,

fever, a very good judge might then be miſtaken ; but a due attention to the nature and violence of the ſymptoms which ſpeedily follow, will ſoon ſet him right.

Now and then there was a little difficulty in making water, but this was merely an accidental ſymptom, and not peculiar to the diſeaſe ; for it often happens after laborious caſes, where the neck of the bladder is ſlightly injured.

The urine was ſmaller in quantity than uſual ; when cold, it was generally reddiſh and high coloured at the beginning of the diſeaſe, and often without the leaſt ſeparation or ſediment ; but as it advanced, there was ſometimes a whitiſh cloud in it, which floated near the ſurface, and when more crude and denſe, ſunk towards the bottom. It was alſo now and then of a whey-color, with a whitiſh oily pellicle on the top, and when it depoſited ſediment, it was generally chalky and not lateritious. But the appearance of urine was continually varying,

varying, and afforded very little information in the cure; for in some of those
where the sediment was copious, though
the bark was immediately administered,
the fever returned and the patient died.

They had very little appetite for food,
and no profound, natural rest; their slum-
bers being disturbed by frequent moaning
and startings; when they waked they seem'd
confused, and not in the least refreshed;
they generally slept with the mouth half
open, and their eyes were imperfectly closed.

A perfect *crisis* seldom ever happened in
this fever; it takes such severe hold of the
constitution at its first onset, that the vital
powers languish, and are unable to produce that salutary event. Indeed, the suppuration of the *omentum*, may be looked
upon as a critical abscess, though of the
unfavorable kind; for it seems to be an unsuccessful endeavour of nature to free herself from the morbid cause; but, wanting
sufficient strength to throw it to the sur-

E

face of the body, it falls upon the interior parts effential to life, and therefore unavoidably becomes mortal.

Sometimes there was a manifeft remiffion of the fymptoms, but where that was not attended with univerfal fweat; or copious difcharge of turbid urine, it was feldom lafting; in fhort, when the fecretions are only partially promoted, the crifis is imperfect, and the patient is fubject to relapfe.

Some of thofe who furvived, recovered very flowly, and were affected with wandering pains and paralytic numbnefs of the limbs, like that of chronic rheumatifm. Some had critical abfceffes in the mufcular parts of the body, which were a long time in coming to fuppuration, and when broke, difcharged fanious ichor; as in the cafe of *Elizabeth Walters.* Others were affected by a flow remitting fever, with great lofs of ftrength and dejection of fpirits; and feveral were fo helplefs and enervated, that they

had

had involuntary ftools a confiderable time after the dangerous fymptoms were over.

When the difeafe proved mortal, the patient generally died on the 10th or eleventh day from the attack: The longeft I have known any one furvive, was *Juliana Thompfon*, who lived fifteen days; and the fhorteft time of being cut off, was in the cafe of *Harriot Truman*, who lived only five days. Moft of them had the clear and diftinct ufe of their fenfes to the laft, and generally expired calmly, without any apparent agony or convulfive ftruggle.

As they became more and more exhaufted, and within a few hours of death; the pulfe, which was exceedingly quick, and almoft imperceptibly weak, at laft was infenfibly loft in a tremulous flutter.

Many authors, particularly the celebrated *Baron Van Swieten*, and *Levret*, fuppofed this fever was occafioned by *metaftafis*, from morbid tranflation of corrupted milk, or

E 2 putrid

putrid obftructed lochia, to the brain, or contents of the thorax and abdomen ; which there produced fuch difeafes as were peculiar to thófe parts, viz. head-ache, vertigo and delirium in the firft ; and in the two laft, inflammation of the lungs, or pleura ; naufea and vomitings, with a diarrhæa and pain in the bowels. Others again with *Hoffman,* imagine that it arifes chiefly from inflammation of the *uterus.*

Thefe have generally been affented to, as the moft probable caufes hitherto affigned, yet it will appear from the following obfervations, they are very exceptionable and inadequate, and not confiftent with the true nature of the difeafe.

To quote a multitude of authors for no other reafon than fhewing their errors, would not only be ufelefs but invidious : I fhall therefore only confider the doctrine of thofe refpectable modern writers aleady mentioned ; and the more particularly,

larly, as their opinions, at this time principally prevail, and have in a manner superceded all the reft.

That the feveral circumftances which are fuppofed to relate to the caufe of this difeafe may become more apparent; it will be neceffary to confider when, and in what manner, the *milk* is ftrained off in the breafts, and what are its qualities when pure, or vitiated; and alfo to attend to the nature of the *lochial difcharge.*

About the third day after delivery, the patient is reftlefs, and complains of a cold, thrilling fenfation towards the back and loins, fucceeded by feverifh heat; the face becomes florid, the pulfe more full and frequent, and at laft the breafts begin to throb and enlarge, by what is ufually called the coming of milk. This flight commotion, or milk fever, which feems to arife from a change of circulation, is generally terminated in the fpace of twenty-four hours, by a warm critical fweat; or if the

F 2 milk

milk is suddenly repelled by diarrhœa, in consequence of which, the febrile symptoms gradually go off.

Van Swieten supposes, that this fever is also partly owing to absorption of *lochia,* which about this time becomes purulent.

Where milk thus secreted is not vitiated by feverish heat of the body, or corrupted by remaining too long in the breasts, it may be absorbed and taken into the blood without any bad consequence ; for milk being nothing but *chyle* exalted and rendered finer by passing through the glands of the breasts, and being the proper nourishment of all animals, it will easily mix with, and be assimilated into *blood*; and since every woman after delivery cannot suckle her child ; Nature has so formed the lactiferous organs as to dispose of milk in this manner, when pure, without injury to the constitution.

If ever therefore, the *Child-bed Fever* is occasioned by a reflux of milk, that can
only

only happen after it has been deprived of its balfamic quality, by too great a degree of animal heat, or ftagnating too long in its veffels: Whereas, this difeafe is fometimes fo fuddenly produced, and attended with fuch remarkable and inftantaneous lofs of ftrength, as appears by a hiftory of the fymptoms, that there is great reafon to believe its firft impreffion is made upon the nerves, or vital powers of the body; and that there is neither fufficient time for the fecretion of milk, or any morbid change of that fluid.

Levret obferves, that this tranflation of milky matter ufually happens, about a fortnight after the difappearance of milk*; and *Van Swieten* afferts, that experience confirms this obfervation +. But could it only be fatisfactorily proved, that fuch tranflation of vitiated milk never happen-

E 4   ed

* L'art des Accouch. p. 150.
+ *Van Swieten*, Commentar. in Her. Boerhaav. Aphor. Vol. iv. p. 610.

ed earlier than the time above mentioned;
it would then fufficiently refute the opinion
of thofe, who fuppofe it the principal
caufe of the difeafe in queftion; fince I
believe, no inftance can be produced where
it came on fo late as the fourteenth day;
for, notwithftanding what *Hippocrates* mentions concerning the wife of *Philinus*, who
was feized with *rigor* on the fourteenth
day after delivery, followed with obftruction of *lochia*; her cafe does not appear
to have been truly fimilar to that under
confideration; a rigor being common to
other fevers as well as that peculiar to
Child-bed Women, and the lochia not
being obftructed in this difeafe.

It cannot be doubted but *milk*, may become depraved by various caufes. Eating
or drinking things which are improper;
expofing the body to cold air; the exceffes
of anger or fear, will often difturb this
fecretion, and occafion milk to ftagnate too
long in the breafts; hence its natural
qualities

qualities may be changed, so as to render it
pernicious ; and consequently, if it should
be re-assumed into the mass of blood in this
vitiated state, it will disorder the body, and
create fever, which however in general, is
soon carried off by some critical evacuation ;
as *diarrhœa*, or *miliary eruption*. But being
too long retained in the lactiferous ducts, it
much oftener brings on abscess of the
breast itself. Such a fever, therefore, is
very essentially different from that under
consideration ; the first being infinitely
more mild in its symptoms, and for the most
part void of danger, for I never yet knew
one die in consequence of it.

Levret also has observed, that were the
milk suddenly disappeared at the beginning
of the disease, and afterward soon returned,
the patient was relieved. But, whenever
this circumstance happens with mitigation
of the symptoms, there is reason to believe
it is owing to a cessation of the febrile cause
which

which no longer interrupts the secretion of that fluid, and which, therefore will naturally return.

When the breasts subside, and the milk gradually goes off, or is suddenly repelled, in those who do not intend to suckle ; the *lochial discharge* may be observed to increase and become more fresh and sanguineous ; and also continues a longer time than in those who do. It therefore appears, that at this time, a plethora prevails in the constitution, which may fall upon the interior vessels, when the milk does not freely pass through the glands of the breasts ; or even should no milk be strained off, the want of it will dispose the habit to a plethoric state. For this reason, women who do not suckle, are visited with a return of the menses, even sometimes so early as in the fifth week after delivery ; whereas, in those who give suck, they are naturally wanting for several months.

Hence

Hence also it is manifest, that the female organs, after a certain age, are so disposed as to prepare a larger quantity of blood than is necessary for the support and nourishment of the body ; which in the time of uterine gestation, is consumed by the foetus, and after delivery, by the child at the breast ; but that this redundant quantity might not incommode the constitution, during the time she is not pregnant ; provident nature has ordered it off by the vessels of the uterus, once every month.

The milk indeed, is not strained off from the blood ; but as the separation of that fluid deprives the woman's body of so much *chyle*, which would otherwise be converted into blood ; the consequence, in respect to her general habit, or the fulness of the vessels, will be exactly the same.

Presuming therefore, that *suckling* after delivery, would lessen the tendency to inflammation and fever, by diminishing the fulness of the uterine vessels, as well as those

of

of the contiguous vifcera ; an order which had formerly been made by the governors of the *Weftminfter Lying-in Hofpital*, at my requeft ; that every patient during her ftay in the houfe, fhould fuckle her child, was at this time, more particularly infifted upon. For if the difeafe was occafioned by tranflation of milk to the interior parts ; it would then follow, that women who had plenty of that fluid, and in whom it was freely difcharged by fuckling, would of all others, be the leaft fubject to it ; but even this caution was infufficient to fecure them from the fever ; for many who had plenty of milk, and fuckled their children, were alfo invaded by it.

But to come to *Practical facts* : In many women, there was a plentiful fecretion of milk, which continued till the fever was confiderably advanced, and fometimes it lafted 'till within a day or two of their death ; in fome few, where the milk was either fmall in quantity, or totally defi

cient,

cient, no fuch fever appeared ; and in thofe cafes where it did, it generally came on before there was any want of milk ; which therefore, was evidently the *effect*, and not the *caufe* of that difeafe.

Befides ; if this fever was owing to a tranflation of milk from the breafts, it would alfo frequently happen to women who wean their children at the end of feven or eight months, which is contrary to experience. The cafe mentioned by *Van Swieten*, of fuch a morbid abforption of that fluid, in a woman a whole year after delivery, in whofe pelvis, *milky matter* was found, only proves what poffibly may, and not what ufually happens.

Indeed from the moft careful examination of the morbid appearances, in the feveral bodies which were opened, I have the greateft reafon to believe, that what has ufually been taken for *coagulated milk*, lying on the furface of the inteftines, is nothing but *pure matter* ; owing to the fuppuration

puration of the *omentum*, and therefore, of a peculiar kind ; having a more white, thick and *curd like appearance*, than that of common matter. As to what is called *ferum lactis*, it feems to be only a purulent whey-coloured fluid, collected in the cavity of the *abdomen*, by *morbid tranfudation* from the inflamed *vifcera* ; or *lymph* become putrid by ftagnating too long there, from a defect in the abforbing power of the lymphatic veffels.

The next principal caufe affigned for the production of this fever, is *obftruction* of *lochia*, and a morbid tranflation of that putrid fluid to the internal parts.

A due attention to the nature of that dif-charge from the *uterus* called *lochia*, which is the natural confequence of delivery, will be moft likely to difcover whether it can have any fhare in producing this fever or not.

As foon as a child is born, the *placenta*, which during pregnancy, ferved as a me-dium

dium of intercourse between the mother
and it, then becomes a lifeless mass without
circulation or further use ; and therefore,
is soon afterwards expelled by the gradual
contraction of the womb. As the separation of this vascular cake from the womb,
is observed to be more easy at the end of
nine months, than in those cases where the
birth is premature ; this animal process
may with reason be supposed analogous
to the dropping off of ripe fruit from a tree.

The *lochia* therefore, is nothing more
than a simple discharge from all those vessels which are torn asunder by the separation of the *placenta* from the *uterus*, and
does not naturally partake of a sanious or
malignant quality, as generally supposed ;
for all the circumstances attending it, exactly correspond with what is observed
to happen after receiving a fresh wound in
any part of the body ; consequently *pure
blood* will first escape from those ruptured
vessels, and afterwards a more dilute and co-
lorless

lorlefs fluid, like the *ferum.* About the
third or fourth day the difcharge generally becomes flightly purulent, and the
uterus contracts, and returns to its unim-
pregnated ftate, the orifices of the feveral
veffels are gradually clofed, and the *lochia*
totally ceafe.

Dr. *Hunter*, by whofe refearches, anato-
mical knowledge has been fo much im-
proved, was the firft who difcovered that
the exterior membrane of the bag containing the child, called *falfe chorion,* is
derived from the *uterus* ; and as it peels off
from thence like a kind of *exuviæ,* or
flough, at each fucceeding birth, he gives
it the name of *membrana decidua.*

By means of the lochial difcharge, the
internal furface of the *uterus* is freed from
the putrid remains of the falfe chorion,
which diffolves and comes away in a fluid
ftate ; and fince there is nothing in its quality but what is common to the digeftion
of a frefh wound ; it is not rational to fuppofe

pofe it can produce a fever fo deftructive to child-bearing women, even allowing it to be obftructed.

I have often obferved the *lochia* fmall in quantity, and at other times redundant, without any bad confequence : This feems chiefly to depend upon the difference of habit in different women, and the lax or tenfe ftate of the uterine fibres ; fo that the indication of danger is not to be taken from the quantity of difcharge, but from the nature of the fymptoms attending it ; and where there is no pain, inflammation, or fever, in the firft cafe, or lofs of ftrength in the laft ; it would be highly improper to direct medicines either to reftrain or promote it.

Befides this error of prefcribing remedies where none are neceffary ; there is another fo prevailing in practice, and fo pernicious in itfelf, that it deferves to be remarked, viz. that of giving *emmenagogue* or uterine medicines, as they are call'd, to promote the *lochia*;

F   for

for thofe being chiefly of the heating kind, as *aloes* and the *pulv. e. myrrh. c.* or elfe fuch as act by their powerful effluvia, as *affafœtid. caftor*, and the like, are fo far from being proper where there is obftruction of this dif-charge, that they are manifeftly injurious, and would be as dangerous to the patient, under fuch circumftances, as forcing medicines given in nephritic cafes, during the height of pain and inflammation. In fhort, all irritating medicines are improper, in every painful or inflammatory affection of the *uterus*, and are therefore to be rejected in favor of gentle evacuations, plentiful dilution, and cooling regimen.

When the *lochial difcharge* becomes fœtid, it has generally been looked upon as a dangerous fign ; but as this often happens without any bad confequence, I am inclined to think, it is rather owing to the ad-miffion of air, into the cavity of the *uterus* and the corruption of grumous blood con-tained there, than to any putrid difpofition

in

in the habit of body; however, it will certainly be right to promote the discharge of such confined *sordes*, as soon as possible; which may be effectually done, by the gentle alternate pressure of the hands applied to the region of the *uterus*, according to the method laid down by *Dusse*.*

Ruysch supposed that the fluid found in the *abdomen*, like the washings of flesh, or corrupted *lochia*, was squeezed from the *uterus*, through the *Fallopian tubes*; + but in all those who were opened I never saw the least quantity of such fluid in the *uterus*, nor could observe any thing to favor so improbable a conjecture.

When the *uterus* was laid open, it had, at first view, the appearance of a part disposed to become *gangrenous*; but this was owing to a considerable quantity of *membrana decidua* or false chorion, adhering to its internal surface; for when I had

F 2　　　　　wiped

* Acad. des Science, l'an. 1724, hist. p. 51.
　+ Observat. Anatom. No. 84. p. 79.

wiped away this mortified flough with a wet fponge, it was perfectly found and in its natural ftate. In the cafe of *Ann Simms* the *os.uteri* was fomewhat livid and blackifh, but as her labor was difficult, this was probably owing to the violence fuftained, and not to any tendency in the difeafe itfelf to produce fuch effect ; for, notwith-ftanding the difcoloration of the part, it did not manifeft the leaft degree of putrid diffolution, but preferved its cohefion and natural firmnefs. It therefore becomes neceffary, not to regard any appearance as morbid, which arifes from accidental caufes, or fuch as are in themfelves ftrictly na-tural.

The fever brought on by *inflammation* of the *uterus*, has often been confounded with Child-Bed Fever : but thofe difeafes are very effentially different, although they both require the fame method of treatment.

When

When the uterus is inflamed, it some-times becomes gangrenous ; the head is af-fected with pain, *delirium* ufually attends the fever, and the uterine region is fo exqui-fitely fenfible, as to render the gentleft preffure intolerable : But on the contrary, in Child-bed Fever, the head is feldom dif-ordered, the *uterus* is not affected with pain, inflammation, or gangrene, nor doth *deli-rium* ufually attend.

Befides thefe general figns of an *inflamed uterus*, there are others more fully men-tioned by *Ætius* than any other writer, which particularly point out the affected parts. When the *fundus uteri* is inflamed, there is great heat, throbbing, and pain above the *pubes* ; if its pofterior part, the pain is more confined to the loins and *rectum*, with *tenefmus* ; if its anterior part, it fhoots from thence towards the neck of the bladder, and is attended with frequent irritation to make water, which is voided

with

with difficulty ; and if its fides or the *ovaria* are affected, the pains will then dart to the infide of the thighs.

- *Inflammation* of the *uterus,* which often arifes from a greater degree of violence applied to this part than its natural ftructure can bear, will generally bring on obftruction of the *lochia* ; and on the other hand, obftruction of *lochia* may produce inflammation of the *uterus* ; but although fuch a local affection may create fever ; it feldom proves mortal, without the inflammation is violent, and terminates in gangrene . In the firft cafe, the orifices of the veffels opening into its cavity, are fhut up, confequently the difcharge will be obftructed, and not return till the tenfion is removed by *bleeding, laxatives,* and *plentiful dilution* ; in the laft, they are fuppofed to be conftricted, and therefore, *opiates* and the *warm bath,* with emollient clyfters will be moft likely to afford relief.

SECTION.

SECTION II.

Practical Observations and Inferences arising from the History of the Disease, respecting its Nature and Cause; with the Methods most conducive to its Cure.

THE sudden change produced in the habit, by the effect of delivery, and that alteration in the course of blood, which must necessarily happen from the contraction of the *uterus*, seem to be the principal reasons why the abdominal viscera, are at this time so liable to *inflammation*.

When the pressure of the gravid uterus is suddenly taken off from the *aorta descendens*, after delivery; the resistance to the impulse of blood passing through all the vessels derived from it, and distributed to the contiguous viscera, will be considerably lessened; it will therefore rush into those vessels with a superior force, and by put-

F 4   ting

ting them violently on the ftretch, may occafion pain, inflammation and fever ; particularly in the *omentum* and *intef- tines*, where they are numerous and moft yielding ; and this is more probable, be- caufe thofe arteries, before they enter the vifcera, are divefted of their ftrong, exter- nal coat.

That fuch a change of circulation actual- ly happens is manifeft from thofe faint- ings which fometimes follow fudden deli- very ; for, when the long continued pref- fure of the uterus is removed ; the blood by gufhing into the inferior veffels, will for a time, deprive the heart and brain of their ufual quantity.

This contraction of the womb, alfo ren- ders its veffels impervious to that blood which before paffed freely through them for the fervice of the child during pregnan- cy ; and confequently a much larger quan- tity will be thrown upon the contiguous parts, which will ftill add to their diften- tion,

tion, and increase their tendency to inflammation; more particularly as the womb
is abundantly supplied with blood, and
receives a greater quantity of veſſels in
proportion to its bulk, than other parts of
the body,

The immoderate ſecretion of *bile*, which
commences about this time, in Child-
bed Fever, moſt probably ariſes from the
ſame cauſe; for, as the *vena portæ ventralis*,
which brings blood to the liver, is rooted
in the inteſtines, it will neceſſarily receive
from thence a larger ſupply than before;
hence a more copious ſecretion, as it is
univerſally allowed, that the quantity of
fluid ſtrained off in any gland, will always be in proportion to the quantity and
velocity of blood paſſing through it.

It therefore appears, that although this
fever is attended with a preternatural ſecretion of bile, it ought not to be conſidered
as one of the bilious kind; for the great
redundancy of that fluid ſeems truely
ſymptomatic

symptomatic, like that occafioned by pain and fpafm in the nephritic colic, or other painful affections of the abdominal vifcera.

At the attack of this fever, the veffels on the furface of the body, during the cold fit, are exceedingly conftricted, as is evident from the palenefs of the fkin ; and from this caufe alfo, a greater quantity of blood is driven to the internal veffels, which will ftill further increafe the quantity of *redundant bile.* Agreeable to this obfervation, the bilious vomiting was generally moft violent after the fhivering fit, or in proportion as that was more or lefs ; and even when it was abated, a return of the cold fit would often bring it on again, as well as the *diarrhœa.*

From this two fold change in the circulation, the veffels of the heart and lungs will alfo receive more blood than before ; hence difficulty of breathing, with anxiety and oppreffion at the breaft, and *præcordia,* which are all relieved by the approach of the

the *hot-fit* ; that is, as foon as the heart re-acts and throws its blood from the centre to the circumference of the body ; and when this cannot be effected, from its want of fufficient power ; the blood will ftagnate in its large contiguous veffels, and the patient will fuddenly expire. Inftances of this fort, though rare, have been known to happen, particularly in the cold fit of an ague, where the attack was uncommonly violent, or in difeafes of the very deftructive kind:

It therefore may be affirmed, that in general, every degree of *rigor* is followed by fever proportionate to it, from the re-action of the heart, which will always be greater or lefs according to the force impreffed upon it by effect of the cold fit ; fo that when it is violent and of long duration, the confequence is much to be feared ; efpecially as nature, by the febrile ftruggle, does not ufually in this difeafe bring on a *falutary crifis*. As the heart now acts ftrongly,

the

the *momentum* of blood on the folids will be greatly increafed, and occafion ten-fion, pain, and inflammation, which, if not foon removed, will end in fuppuration of the internal parts, and produce a *collection of matter* in the cavity of the *abdomen*, from which it cannot be evacuated, and there-fore inevitably muft become mortal.

If the preceding reafoning be right, it will fhew the neceffity of attempting to di-minifh the cold fit, by the plentiful ufe of diluting fluids given warm; and alfo of hot applications to the extremities and furface of the body, to relax the cutaneous veffels, and invite the blood thither, fo as to relieve thofe of the *viscera* from diftention; for whatever is the caufe of this fever, its firft impreffion feems to be made upon the nerves, which leffens their influence on the body, and prevents that free and equal diftribution of blood neceffary to a ftate of health.

To anfwer this intention, I would prefer an infufion of any of the grateful aromatic

vegetables

vegetables given warm, as that of mint, fage, or elder flowers, rather than fluids of the spirituous kind ; for, by their heating quality, they increafe the violence of the hot fit or fubfequent fever, which is the principal thing to be guarded againft ; whereas the former may be given at difcretion, fo as only to act during the *rigor*, and will afterwards become of fervice in abating the febrile fymptoms by their diluting and refolvent power.

This tendency to inflammation will be moft likely to produce violent effects after delivery, when the abdominal vifcera are in a tender irritable ftate, both from that change of circulation already mentioned, which for a time, will render the woman's conftitution weak and valetudinary, as well as the violent efforts of labour itfelf. That particular parts of the body are more difpofed to inflammation, as the habit changes and becomes more irritable, is evident from repeated obfervation ; for inftance, in

cafes

cafes of a ftone in the bladder, the pain and inflammation are not continual, but only produced at particular periods from fome accidental exciting caufe, which at that time renders the affected part more fenfible.

As long as the folids of the body continue in their natural ftate, they will allow of being ftretched to a certain degree without pain ; but as foon as they become inflamed or difeafed, the leaft irritation or diftending caufe will bring on the moft intolerable fenfations ; and this feems to be the reafon why air or fœces contained in the bowels, at one time produce exceffive pain, and at another none at all.

Hence alfo a complication of this fever, with *pleurify* or *peripneumouy* ; and fometimes a delirium, phrenfy, or madnefs attend, where the blood is more immediately determined to the brain, by anxiety, grief, or other caufes which occafion intenfe exercife of mind. Three cafes of this

this kind have occurred to me, in all which the diſeaſe was fatal ; one of them was that of a baker's wife in *Weſtminſter*, who remained well till the fourth day after delivery, but being ſuddenly diſturbed with ſome religious ſcruples, ſhe was violently ſeized with this fever, attended with delirium, which carried her off ; notwithſtanding the uncommon attention paid to her ſafety, by an eminent phyſician, who was called in at my requeſt, and with whom I wiſhed to have conſulted, but was accidentally prevented, by being called another way.

Dr. *Hales*, in his curious Hæmaſtatical Experiments, clearly demonſtrates, that the blood's impulſe on its containing veſſels is exceedingly increaſed by the violent action of the muſcles, particularly thoſe of the abdomen ; he alſo remarks, that air retained in the lungs after a deep inſpiration, has the ſame effect ; and ſince the birth of a child is brought about by a

combination

combination of muscular forces, viz. from that of the uterus, assisted by the action of the very muscles already mentioned ; namely those of the abdomen and diaphragm, the last of which is pressed down on the inferior parts, at every deep inspiration ; it becomes evident, that violent stress is laid upon the vessels of the abdominal viscera, even in those labours which are strictly natural. Such are the effects of labour-pains on the whole vascular system, that the pulse which before was temperate and regular, becomes full and frequent ; the complexion florid, and sometimes the face is enormously swelled, by the violent efforts and straining of the body. Till such a change is produced, women are not subject to this fever; for I observed, that those with child, who assisted the nurses in attending the sick, were perfectly free from it, even when it was most rife ; *but being delivered, several of them sickened soon after, and were affected with the same symptoms*

as

as the reft. This difeafe cannot therefore, with propriety, be called by any other name than *puerperal* or *Child-bed Fever.* Had a modern Author been acquainted with this *ftriking fact*, he would not probably have cavilled at the appellation. May not this circumftance added to that change of circulation already remarked, and to the great fenfibility and irritability of habit obferved to prevail after delivery, concur as fo many exciting caufes to kindle up this fever ? and alfo fhew, why women are never fubject to it before, *but only after delivery*; and more particularly, during an unhealthy conftitution of the atmofphere. For if this difeafe was owing to *compreffion of the abdominal vifcera* in general, or to that of the *omentum* in particular, independent of any alteration in the air, as fome have afferted ; fince this caufe is the fame in all gravid women, its confequences would alfo be more uniform, and the difeafe would be equally frequent at all times

G

of

of the year, inftead of prevailing with un-common violence at particular feafons. Be-fides, if it was occafioned by preffure of the gravid uterus on the contiguous vifcera ; it would *neceffarily happen before delivery, when that preffure was greateft* ; whereas, expe-rience fhews that it never appears 'till after delivery, even in the *epidemical feafon.* In fhort, if pregnancy produced this fever, pregnant women would be fubject to it, and delivery, by emptying the uterus, *would not occafion but cure it* ; according to that univerfal axiom, take away the caufe, and the effect will ceafe.

The vital powers of the vifcera being thus impaired, their feveral functions will be unduly performed, particularly the *ab-forption of lymph* from the abdominal cavity ; hence depravity and corruption of that re-tained ftagnating fluid, and an increafe of pain and inflammation of thofe parts with which it is in contact; hence alfo fwell-ing of the belly, which may be looked upon

as

as a *species of tympanites*. This morbid affection did not seem to happen from wind in the bowels ; for, if so, it would have subsided, by the frequency of stools, which was not the case. It was evidently owing to expansion of air generated in the cavity of the abdomen, from putrid dissolution of the *omentum*, and a corruption of purulent fluid collected there in large quantities.

The dissection of bodies thus affected, confirmed me in this opinion ; for, on cutting into the *abdomen*, a putrid *flatus*, intolerable to the smell, issued forth with a hissing noise, and the prominence of the belly immediately subsided. In general, there was but little air in the intestines, which were likewise almost empty of *fæces*, and only contained a blackish fluid like that voided by stool, with particles of something which looked like fat after it had been melted and become cold.

Considering the suppuration of *omentum*, and large quantity of purulent fluid found

in

in the *abdomen* after death ; it is eafy to fee how a fever which was truly *inflammatory* in the beginning, may foon become *putrid*, by abforption of that fluid, which like *old leven*, will taint the blood, and by exciting a putrid ferment in the whole mafs, change its qualities into thofe of its own morbid nature.

The ftructure and ufe of the *lymphatics*, and their exiftence as a diftinct fyftem of veffels, numeroufly diftributed to the feveral cavities of the body, difcovered and accurately defcribed by Dr. *Hunter*, with experiments made on quadrupedes, fufficiently demonftrate the reality of this abforption ; for it has often been obferved, that although a large quantity of any warm fluid had been injected into the abdominal cavity of different animals in the living ftate, not a drop of it could be found after death.

Befides,

Befides, as the *liver* chiefly receives its blood from the inteftines, *omentum*, and *mefentery*, which is loaded with *oil*, abforbed by the veins from the two laft parts, fo as to render it fitter for the fecretion of *bile* ; it will follow, that, as foon as the *omentum* is deftroyed by putrid diffolution ; the refluent blood carried to the liver will be vitiated and corrupted, and paffing through that large gland to mix with the general mafs, will contaminate the whole, and produce a true *febris purulenta.* Hence general inflammation, adhefions of the lungs and *pleura* ; a collection of putrid *ferum* in the *thorax*, and matter under the *fternum* ; as in the cafe of *Harriot Trueman.* This appears more probable, becaufe, on enquiry of the patient's friends, I could not find fhe had ever been in the leaft fubject to any complaint in the breaft. Befides, as *bile*, of all the humors in the body, is moft liable to be changed, this fluid, tainted with blood brought from the *dif-*

eafed

eafed omentum, will foon become putrid, and
by its cauftic acrimony create anxiety, ficknefs, and vomiting, with *tormina* in the
bowels, and profufe *diarrhæa* ; fo that it
will now offend in quality, as well as quantity, which laft has already been fufficiently taken notice of. Before it is altered from
its natural ftate, it feems in a great meafure
inoffenfive to the ftomach ; becaufe frefh,
infpiffated bile of animals, given as a medicine, does not occafion the above diforders.

Thus I think it evidently appears, that
the fymptoms of putrefaction were not originally fuch, but are produced by *metaflafis* ;
not from that of *vitiated milk* or *obftructed
lochia,* as generally fuppofed ; but by abforption of *purulent fluids* ftagnating in the
abdomen, and morbid tranflation of matter
from the *fuppurated omentum* ; and if ever
marks of putrefaction appear in the beginning, they are confined to the *primæ viæ*
only, and arife from tainted, rancid bile ;
for a corruption of the blood and juices never

ver happens till in the advanced ftate of this difeafe ;. otherwife, fuch a putrefactive tendency in the habit would certainly exert itfelf fooner, and produce the difeafe before delivery; efpecially in the *epidemic* feafon.

As foon as internal mortification commences, the pain ceafes, which perfuades thofe prefent that the patient is better ; but when this fuddenly happens, after it has been exceffive a confiderable time, and in an advanced ftate of the difeafe, without any critical evacuation which could prove falutary, it is a fatal and delufive fign, and foon followed by a finking, quick and intermitting pulfe, fwelling of the belly, a diftreffed countenance, with partial, faint fweats on the breaft and face, and fometimes by dilirium, which fhew that death is at hand.

That acute and incomparable practical phyfician *Baglivi*, was the firft who de-

fcribed

scribed the *mesenteric fever*, and obferves, that latent inflammations of the vifcera, are generally the caufe of thofe fevers called malignant, and which often end in abfcefs or gangrene of the affected parts, when *bleeding* has been neglected.

In painful or inflammatory difeafes of the vifcera, fo great is the fenfibility of the feveral parts, that the whole nervous fyftem is eafily drawn into confent ; hence a perverfion or defect of their feveral natural functions. The heart will be affected with fpafm, and not being able duly to perform its office, the pulfe will become quick, weak, and intermitting. This dimunition of nervous influence on the affected internal parts, will alfo account for the great and fudden lofs of ftrength, and fhew why the *pulfe* is *weak, quick* and *irregular* in Child-bed Fever, inftead of being hard and full, as in the pleurify ; and indeed, in moft difeafes of the abdominal vifcera, the pulfe becomes languid, and lofes it firmnefs, be-

fore

fore there can be any actual proſtration of bodily ſtrength ; as in caſes of taking poiſon, or where a violent fit of gout ſuddenly fixes upon the vital parts.

As it appears that women, ſo long as they remain with child, are not more ſubject to this fever, than others who are not pregnant ; it will follow, that a diſtemperature of air is not alone ſufficient to produce it, until it is aſſiſted by change of habit in conſequence of delivery ; but as ſuch a change is then common to all women, it is alſo evident, that in general, it may be endured without much danger, whilſt the ſeaſon remains healthy ; ſince ſcarce one in a thouſand is then affected with it ; except from *errors* in *diet*, *paſſions* of the *mind*, the effect of *taking cold*, or other manifeſt, exciting cauſes ; conſequently, it will always be found moſt ſevere, whenever ſuch concurring cauſes are moſt numerous, and in proportion as they are more or leſs dangerous in their own nature : Thus for inſtance,

ftance, it will always be found moft *fatal*
when moft *epidemical*, that is, during a diftemperature of the air ; and leaft of all fo,
when it happens in healthy feafons, from
accidental caufes only. If at fuch a time,
it fhould arife fimply from taking cold, it
is often terminated by a profufe, long continued fweat ; if from food offending the
ftomach in quantity or quality, the patient
is often relieved by fpontaneous vomiting or
a diarrhæa ; but on the contrary, if it is
brought on by the violent paffions of the
mind, the event is different ; for as the
caufe continues, fo does the fever likewife.
Befides, in fuch cafes, there is generally a
defect in the natural fecretions and excretions, and as nothing will weaken the vital
powers of body fo much as diftrefs of mind ;
a falutary crifis is then very feldom known
to happen.

I have alfo obferved, that this
difeafe generally comes on about the fecond or third day after delivery, and that
the

the fooner it attacks the patient, the more she is in danger. The fenfibility and irritability of body, which are always obferved greateft at that time, feem to account for the firft of thefe circumftances, and alfo fhew why the fever is then moft dangerous in its event ; feeing, that this predifpofing caufe exifting in the habit, will then moft powerfully co-operate with, or increafe the agency of any other external caufe, which may chance to occur.

From this preceding hiftory of the *Child-Bed Fever*, joined to its morbid appearances already mentioned ; the following conclufions may be drawn by way of recapitulation.

Firft, that it does not arife from a tranflation of · *corrupted milk*, or *obftructed lochia* ; fecondly, that it is not owing to *iuflammation* of the *uterus* ; thirdly, that a certain *mecanical change* produced in the body by delivery, is the principal predifpo-'

fing

fing cause of the disease, and the reason why it is *peculiar to women after delivery only* ; fourthly, that whenever it is remarkably frequent and fatal at particular seasons, its proximate cause ought to be referred to a *noxious constitution of the air* ; which was still more fully proved by those cases, where the fever suddenly appeared in the epidemic season, without any other evident cause whatsoever. Fifthly, that it may sometimes happen in the most healthy seasons, from the *accidental causes* already enumerated, and that in such instances, it is least dangerous ; sixthly, that the temporary change brought upon the habit, by delivery, may generally be endured without producing this fever, if none of the causes already mentioned then happen to supervene ; and also that women are more or less subject to the impression of all such causes, in proportion to the sensibility and irritability of their habit : Lastly, that it is not owing to the pressure of the *gra-*

vid

vid uterus on the *abdominal viscera* in general, or the *omentum* in particular ; for if so,
pregnant women would be more subject to
it, than those lately delivered, confequently it could not be *Child-bed Fever.*

I have been more diffuse in what relates
to the *Pathology* of this difeafe, becaufe, nothing will tend fo much to eftablifh a rational method of cure, as thofe *obfervations
which immediately refult from the difeafe
itfelf; the ftructure and ufe of the feveral affected parts, and their morbid appearances after
death.*

In the *Child-bed Fever,* therefore, as well
as all thofe, which like it, are truely inflammatory, and uniformly produce *internal
fuppuration*; *bleeding* is the only remedy
which can give the patient a chance for
life ; efpecially, as local inflammation, if
violent, more frequently terminates by a
fatal fuppuration than any other way,
where that has been neglected.

Indeed,

Indeed, from the strictest attention to the several symptoms and circumstances of this disease; without shaping a theory to coincide with any particular method of practice ; the reasons for bleeding are as manifest and cogent as in the *pleurify* itself, where an *empyema* is sometimes brought on ; for a collection of matter in the thorax or abdomen are equally fatal.

The principal objections by those who are averse to bleeding, are as follow. Considering the loss of blood after delivery, and subsequent lochial discharge, it would exhaust the patient's strength too much, especially as she is usually enjoined abstemious diet for several days after ; that by lessening the strength, it would prevent a crisis ; increase irritability of the body, and aggravate all the symptoms of this fever, or dispose it to become putrid. But those are groundless objections and plainly contradicted by what may be observed in practice ; for the violence of fever,

and

and *symptomatic purging* arifing from it, will be found to fink the patient's ftrength much more than lofs of blood, which, on the contrary, by removing tenfion and pain from the bowels which act as a ftimulus and keep up the diarrhœa, will have the effect of an *anodyne*, and more fafely abate that difcharge than either opiates or aftringents, both which are highly improper at the beginning of the difeafe. *Bleeding*, by diminifhing the quantity, and force of the blood through the liver, and larger internal veffels, will likewife leffen the *fecretion of bile*, and therefore relieve the ficknefs and anxiety at ftomach, as well as difficulty of breathing and oppreffion of the *præcordia*.

Befides, I am inclined to think that women after delivery, efpecially thofe who do not fuckle, are able to bear the lofs of blood much better, than is generally imagined ; for as the fœtus does not then demand its long-accuftomed fupply of nourifhment,

rifhment, it will revert to the mother, and gradually create a temporary plethora, as already obferved.

It ought alfo to be remarked, that neither *inanition* or *plethora* are natural to the body in a healthy ftate ; that one extreme is hurtful as the other, and will produce irritation in as high a degree ; for in plethoric habits, where the veffels are overcharged and violently upon the ftretch, all the fymptoms of irritability are evidently increafed. The fame quantity of light which did not offend the eye in its natural ftate, becomes intolerable to it when inflamed ; and the ear is not able to endure the leaft noife, without being difagreeably affected, after being feized with inflammation.

To proceed, *early and copious bleeding*, at the onfet of the difeafe, will prove much more ferviceable than afterwards ; thus, eight, or ten ounces of blood taken away at firft, will afford more relief than

twice

twice that quantity at different times. By the firſt method, tenſion of the veſſels is ſuddenly taken off, and the *pain, fever*, and *inflammation* are thereby abated. The whole vaſcular ſyſtem being now relieved, a more free and equal diſtribution of the blood will follow, and the natural ſecretions being more duly performed, a *ſalutary criſis* may the rather be expected. On the contrary, where the veſſels have remained long on the ſtretch, and being as it were overſtrained, have loſt their reſiſting power, all the above ſymptoms will be increaſed ; and although blood ſhould at laſt be drawn, if the inflammatory ſymptoms have run high, and *matter has begun to form in the omentum, or any of the vital parts, from which it cannot be evacuated ; it is then too late to expect relief* ; for the diſeaſe muſt neceſſarily become fatal, both by a diſſolution of parts eſſential to life, and the confinement of that purulent fluid, which will not only corrupt and deſtroy the ſurrounding *viſcera*,

H   but

but by its abforption will foon taint the whole fluid mafs ; fo that although bleeding in the beginning, is the principal remedy to be depended on, it will *feldom prove of fervice after the fecond or third day* of the attack ; and if directed later, will only further exhauft and enfeeble the patient, and haften her end.

Confidering the languid ftate of the patient, and weaknefs of her pulfe, even in the beginning of this fever, I was furprized to find the inflammation had fometimes run fo high and made fuch rapid progrefs, as to produce matter in the abdomen, fo early as the *fourth* or *fifth day* after the firft attack, as will appear in the cafe of *Harriot Trueman* ; which fully proves the neceffity of bleeding *early,* or *not at all.*

Practitioners, from a fcrupulous attention to their reputation, are generally fparing in the application of fuch remedies as have been doubted in their good effects, by thofe of the profeffion, or even where vulgar

gar prejudices have been violent in oppofing their ufe. It is no wonder therefore, confidering the weaknefs of pulfe fo remarkable in this fever, with the objections already mentioned, that *bleeding* fhould have been directed with an uncommon degree of caution, for where blood was drawn at all, it was only in *trifling quantities, aud feldom till the decline of the difeafe,* where every thing elfe had been tried in vain ; and confequently where *matter being formed,* neither that evacuation, nor any other human means, could poffibly avail. Thus, the mifapplication of this remedy, plainly appears to have been the reafon why it was not fooner adopted as fafe and beneficial.

In fhort, as no *purulent matter* can be formed without *preceding inflammation* ; and as no means have hitherto been found fo effectual in abating inflammation, as *bleeding, laxatives,* and *plentiful dilution* ; thofe, who cannot fee the abfolute neceffity for their ufe, muft certainly fhut their eyes on all conviction. H 2 As

As the cure will be found to depend principally on the feasonable lofs of blood ; it will be requifite to regard all fuch indications as may be taken from the *pulfe*, and to lay down fuch rules and cautions as particularly relate to this circumftance.

Nothing will fo clearly point out the time when this remedy ought to be directed, as a previous acquaintance with the natural ftate of the pulfe, which is found to vary exceedingly in different habits of body : A difference in the fize and diftribution of the artery conftituting the pulfe, will alfo occafion very different impreffions on the finger in regard to its ftrength or weaknefs ; confequently, it ought to be alternately felt in each arm of the fame perfon. The general habit, age, and manner of living, will alfo afford great information in this particular ; for inftance, if the patient is young, and previoufly enjoyed an uninterrupted ftate of health, with a keen appetite and good digeftion ; when the pulfe

in

in such a person seems to sink in the very beginning; such a sudden alteration arises from oppression, and not weakness, and requires immediate loss of blood; particularly, where no profuse evacuation had preceded, such as hæmorrhage, diarrhæa, or long abstinence, anxiety of mind, with want of rest, or great bodily fatigue. On the contrary, if she has been of a valetudinary, hysterical habit, with lax fibres, bad digestion and pale aspect; a languid pulse, with such appearances, may reasonably be imputed to a real want of bodily strength rather than oppression; and consequently, bleeding ought to be omitted.

We are also told, that on compressing the artery at the wrist, with the finger, if from being small and apparently weak, it suddenly becomes more strong and renitent; we may be sure it is oppression, and not weakness, which then prevails. This, however, I think, is not an opinion well founded; for whether the artery beats languidly

H 3   from

from real weaknefs, or the diminifhed impulfe of the heart, or whether the action of
the arterial fyftem is overcome by too great
a plenitude of veffels ; the effect will be
nearly the fame in both cafes, and the artery will act weakly on the touch.

The degree of ftrength may be better
known by attending to the more obvious
figns of ftrength or weaknefs, and by regarding the flownefs or frequency of
pulfe ; for, in proportion as bodily ftrength
is exhaufted, it increafes in frequency ; and
on the contrary, when the ftrength remains unimpaired, the number of pulfations
are proportionably lefs ; but being both
more full and ftrong, the circulation is then
more uniformly carried on than when the
artery beats quicker ; for the free diftribution of blood through its veffels, does not
depend upon the frequency of the heart's
contraction, but on the degree of ftrength
and energy with which it acts at each pulfation.

But

But the moſt ſecure way of proceeding in doubful caſes, will be to feel the pulſe during the time that blood is flowing from the vein ; if its ſtrokes become more ſtrong, ample and free, the quantity to be taken away may be increaſed ; but if it ſinks and loſes its equality and firmneſs, the bleeding orifice ſhould immediately be cloſed. However care is to be taken, leſt we are impoſed upon by that languor of the pulſe, brought on by compreſſion of the artery, by an over-tightneſs of ligature round the arm.

It was neceſſary to be more particular on this head, as there is great difference between *nature oppreſſed*, and *nature exhauſted* ; and as the ſafety of the patient principally depends upon a true diſtinction between real want of ſtrength, and that which is only apparently ſo.

Without we are previouſly acquainted with the natural ſtate of the pulſe, and its number of ſtrokes in a minute, when the

H 4 body

body is in health; little information can be had when we are told it beats a hundred and twenty, or any certain number of strokes in a minute, during the time of difeafe. I have therefore, in the hiftory of the cafes which follow, rather chofen to fignify the degree of feverifh heat, by the general terms of weak and ftrong, quick or flow, as applied to the pulfe, than by mentioning the precife number of its ftrokes in a minute.

From thefe preceding general Obfervations, the indication of cure may be taken. Hence it will follow, that *bleeding* ought to be directed at the *very onfet of the difeafe*; fecondly, that it will be neceffary to diminifh the violence and duration of the *cold fit*; thirdly, the redundant, *corrupted bile* is to be evacuated and corrected as foon as poffible; fourthly, that the *diarrhœa*, when exceffive, ought to be reftrained by emollient, anodyne clyfters, and gentle fudorifics, or even by opiates, and mild aftringents,

gents, when the patient's strength begins to sink under the long-continued discharge; and lastly, where signs of *putrefaction*, or an *intermission* of the fever appear; that antiseptics and *Peruvian bark* may be freely administered.

The choice of remedies is often matter of great difficulty, even to those most conversant with the nature of diseases, and after that is determined, it is not so much the medicine itself, as its application, which renders it truly salutary; for as things derive their value from their proper use, so efficacious medicines injudiciously administered, like blessings perverted, are of all others *most dangerous*; since whatever is powerfully good, if properly given, will become as powerfully bad, when misapplied.

As it is of great use to discover by fair trial, what medicines are principally to be depended upon in the cure of particular diseases; so it would be highly serviceable if
those

those in practice, conscious of their own upright intention, would also venture, candidly to point out such methods and medicines, as they had found either *useless* or *prejudicial.*

Dutean and the French writers in general are great advocates for the use of *Camphor* in the cure of this disease ; and Dr. *Störck,* who seems to have copied them, recommends its liberal use in a mixture of Peruvian Bark. For common drink he also directs the almond emulsion with one dram of Camphor to every pint ; and clysters to be injected twice a day, with one dram of Camphor dissolved in broth by the assistance of Gum Arabic. From this method and the omission of blood-letting, he tells us that all his patients happily recovered. Happily indeed, if such was the event ! For my own part, being honestly solicitous for the safety of my patients, and the improvement of medicine, rather than the establishment of particular doctrines, I should

should rejoice to find the success of this method verified by the *test of future experience*, which alone will best determine its effects. I confess, however, my doubts at so general an assertion, especially when I look back on the fate of *Extract. Cicutæ*, after being usher'd into practice with such extravagant encomiums by the same author.

As I have chiefly taken these remarks from the second part of the *Foreign Medical Review*, I think it proper to conclude them in the words of the author of that publication, as follows :

" If what the author (*Störck*) here relates be true, this method would doubtless be preferable to any other ; and his veracity in this point, may, we think, be determined by those who have the inspection of Lying-in Hospitals. We shall only remark, that all medical books published at Vienna, iu which Dr. *Störck*, or whoever presides over the faculty, are so much flattered,

flattered, as to render us fufpicious, in refpect to the truth of the obfervations they contain."

In general, I think too much is attempted by medicines ; and as their proper application requires fkill, fo it ought no lefs to be deemed true medical knowledge, to determine when it is better to ftand ftill, and watch the operations of Nature, rather than to proceed in the dark, and run the rifk of thwarting her falutary endeavours. By fuch means fome difeafes either become tedious in the cure, if. happily they are cured at all ; which in a manner left to themfelves, or treated by fimple remedies, would perhaps be terminated more favorably ; efpecially where the habit of body is good, the vifcera found, and the natural fecretions neither greatly defective or perverted.

Nothing can be more blameable than that precipitate and defultory method of flying from one medicine to another, at the

the appearance of every new symptom ; without waiting sufficient time to observe the effects of any ; it is indeed prescribing for the *symptoms only*, instead of the cause of the disease from which they spring; and is not acting more rationally than he who should attempt to clear his garden of weeds by only plucking off their leaves.

In regard to loss of blood, the quantity to be taken away is not so much to be determined by its appearance, as the degree of pain, fever, and difficulty of breathing; for its *sizness* is not uncommon in *pregnant women*, even in a state of health ; and in diseases of the inflammatory kind, it seems to be the consequence, and not the cause of inflammation ; for the first-drawn blood is seldom ever so sizy as that taken away after continuance of the fever.

When the patient is young and plethoric, the pulse full, thirst great, the skin dry, and the urine high colored ; she may lose eight or ten ounces of blood, in the beginning

ning, with great safety and advantage;
and a smaller quantity may afterwards be
repeatedly taken away, in proportion to the
violence of the symptoms.

Large draughts of warm tea, or any
other diluting liquor may then be given,
and afterwards, bladders half full of hot
water may be wrapped in flannels and applied to the soles of the feet, the *axillæ* and
sides, in order to lessen the violence of the
cold fit, and keep up the circulation in the
extremities and surface of the body, where
it is most languid.

One would have imagined that the
warm bath bid fairer to answer this intention than any thing else, as it acts like a
universal fomentation applied to the bodily
surface; and the rather, since it has been
found to procure almost instant ease in other
disorders of the bowels; but to the confu-
sion of all theory, in those cases where it
was tried, it by no means answered my expectation; and from what I could learn,
                                    succeeded

fucceeded no better with others; for the greateft part of thofe died for whom it was directed: This however, in fome meafure, might be owing to want of bleeding, which was generally neglected in the beginning; or becaufe, like that, it was made ufe of too late, viz. after the *formation of matter* in the abdomen.

Upon the whole, the warm bath, by firft acting as a refolvent, from abforption of aqueous particles into the blood, will footh the nerves, relax the fkin and enlarge the pores, and therefore, tend to promote a free perfpiration, without heating the body; and as I am ftill inclined to think favorably of it, when feafonably applied after bleedings, could wifh to recommend it as a remedy which deferves further trial.

When it is thought neceffary, a bathing tub near two parts full of warm water, may be placed at the patient's bedfide, into which fhe may be gently lifted, and fuffered

to

to remain for ten, fifteen minutes, or longer
if she does not grow faint ; when taken out,
a clean, warm sheet may instantly be applied all over her body, to spunge up the
moisture ; after which, a loose flannel gown,
long enough to come down to her feet,
may be put on warm next her skin, and
draughts of any thin diluting fluid may
then be given in bed, to promote persp-
piration. The bath should only be of
a temperate heat, otherwise, instead of
relaxing, it will crisp the fibres of the
skin, and defeat the purposes for which
it was intended.

To evacuate offending bile from the stomach, nothing proved more effectual than
the following *emetic* :

 ℞. *Tart. emet. gr. ii.*

   Aq. alex. simp. ℥ ifs

   Oxymel. Scillit. ℥ *iii misce.*

It acted much sooner than *ipecacoanha*, and
did not bring on such intolerable and long-
continued sickness after its first operation ;

         which

which perhaps might be owing to a more perfect solution of antimony by the acidity of oxymel; it also seems to possess a febrifuge quality, and disposes the patient to sweat; an effect probably arising from what is common to other emetics which produce that effect by agitating the body.

When the nausea and sickness are violent, the emetic should be weaker; but if the stomach is scarcely affected, it may then be wholly omitted, and a *gentle laxative* given after bleeding, which will procure a free discharge of bile.

Bleeding ought generally to precede the emetic for reasons already given; and also because the abdominal viscera will suffer less from the efforts of vomiting when the vessels are more empty.

After most of the bile has been rejected, by spontaneous vomiting, or the emetic draught; the putrescence, or rancid acrimony of what remains,

I should

should also be corrected. Acefcent vegetable juices feemed moft likely to anfwer this intention ; as thofe of oranges, lemons, &c. I therefore, at firft directed them in draughts of weak tea, or barley water ; but fuch was the tendernefs and irritability of the inteftines, that, by the continuance of this method, the patient would foon have been purged to death ; confequently they were immediately laid afide. We alfo tried the *faline mixture*, where the acid was exactly neutralized, and which, on many accounts, promifed fair for a ufeful medicine ; but that likewife proved fo purgative, that it could feldom be fafely continued without the addition of *fperm. ceti* and *gum. arab.* which rendered it more foft and friendly to the bowels ; although even this alteration was not always fufficient to remedy the inconvenience complained of.

The following draught, which is purpofely directed in a fmaller quantity than ufual, may be given every four or five hours, or at any time as occafion requires.

Sperm.

℞ *Sperm. Ceti*
Mucilag. Gum Arab. aa ℥ ſs *bene*
tritis & ſubactis, ſenſim adde
Succ. Limon. ℥ ſs, *cum*
Sal. Abſinth. ſaturat.
Aq. Cinnamon. Simp. ℥ i
Syr. balſamic. ℥ i, *miſce.*

Saline mixture given in a ſtate of efferveſcence has ſometimes been known to ſtop the moſt violent bilious vomitings, where every thing elſe had been tried in vain.

The frothing or conflict which ariſes on mixing the acid and alkali, ſeems more properly ebullition than fermentation ; yet there is reaſon to believe the effect of this medicine given as above, is produced by ſomething ſimilar to what the Chymiſts call *Gas Sylveſtre*, or the effluvia eſcaping from fermenting liquors, which will ſweeten and reſtore fleſh that was become putrid and ſtinking.

I 2   So

So powerfully antiseptic is this *subtile gas*, that we are told, the plague at *Marseilles* was stopped by its influence ; for that dreadful calamity suddenly ceased soon after the *vintage* ; owing, as was supposed, to the vapors arising from the vast quantities of *fermenting new wines* made there.

Where this fever proceeds from the violent passions of mind, and attacks those of plethoric habits attended with *delirium* ; an emetic would be very improper ; half an ounce of lemon-juice, in a tea-cup full of water, may therefore, be given, upon which, a scruple of sal absinth. dissolved in the same quantity, may be drank immediately after ; so as to produce an effervescence in the stomach, from which none of the subtile effluvia can escape ; and therefore it will still more effectually answer the intention of correcting the corrupted bile, especially if the alkaline salt is allowed to predominate ; for the process of sweet-

sweetening and purifying *rancid train oil* depends chiefly upon its antiseptic principle.

This mixture will also evacuate gently by stool, which is more necessary, where no emetic has previously been given.

Those who direct medicines in this disease are extremely divided in their opinion concerning the diarrhæa ; being in doubt whether it is *critical, or symptomatic*. An evacuation happening so early as to usher in the disease, cannot properly be considered otherwise than *symptomatic*, as I have already endeavoured to shew ; but wherever the case appears perplexing, the best and surest way will be to keep a watchful eye on the patient ; if she is much relieved by the appearance of this, or any other discharge, it never ought suddenly to be suppressed ; but on the contrary, if the symptoms, which before prevailed, either continue without mitigation, or are aggravated ; and above all, if her strength

I 3 begins

begins hourly to fink and decline ; fuch an evacuation fhould fpeedily be reftrained of totally taken away, if it is in the power of medicine to do it ; without lofing time in making finical diftinctions, more ingenious than ufeful : But however fimple and obvious this practical obfervation may appear, it has not been fufficiently attended to.

When the diarrhæa is *truly critical*, which is feldom the cafe, it commences later ; the ftools have more confiftence and are of a yellowifh hue, the belly is foft, appetite and fleep return, and the patient is much relieved. On the contrary, in the *fymptomatic diarrhæa* ; the ftools are black and flimy, at laft becoming watery, and sometimes of a dark olive-color, or like that of rufty iron ; thirft and fever continue, and the belly is tenfe and painful,

But altho' the diarrhæa is not ftrictly critical, it manifeftly affords relief in the early ftate of the difeafe, and thereforeought not to be ftopped by *opiates or aftringents,* which

which I found injurious, especially in strong plethoric habits, where bleeding had been neglected : By constipating the bowels, they concentrate the sordes collected there, and if the purging does not return ; great oppression at stomach will follow, with increase of thirst, sickness and nausea : In short, whenever these medicines are thus unseasonably administered, they will always be attended with the worst consequences, and aggravation of all the feverish symptoms, as I had frequent opportunities of observing.

On the contrary, when the body is kept laxative, the intestines are unloaded of their putrid contents ; sickness and oppression are relieved, and the fever is considerably abated.

Emollient clysters prepared from fresh animal substances, should next be frequently administered, and the longer they remain with the patient, so much the better, as they will then more effectually cherish the

I 4

bowels

bowels by their gentle warmth and relaxing vapor, and act as internal fomentations to the whole abdominal viscera; besides, by being abforbed, they will dilute the blood and become refolvent.

Seven or eight ounces of chicken or beef water, or a weak decoction of chicken guts, without fat, falt, or any other addition, will anfwer the purpofe; but all fuch clyfters fhould only be given milk-warm, and in fmall quantity, otherwife they will diftend the inteftines, and by creating pain will foon be forced away.

Whenever the bowels are affected with pain, *opiates*, after evacuations, are beft given in clyfters; being then immediately applied as it were to the naked nerves of the difeas'd part; hence they diminifh irritability of the inteftines, relieve pain, procure fleep, and are lefs liable to affect the head, than when given by the mouth: Thus, g^{tt}. xxxx of *tinct. thebaic.* may be added, as occafion requires,

Clyfters

Clyfters of the cathartic kind, are alfo neceffary before the ufe of purgatives, when the patient has been long coftive; for where the laft have been given and do not readily pafs off; fevere gripings and tormina will follow.

Some are fo timorous, that they will not venture to give *laxatives* 'till the fourth or fifth day after delivery, left they fhould check the *lochial difcharge*, or bring on a dangerous purging; but thefe are unneceffary cautions, for I never knew the *lochia* niterrupted, nor any diarrhæa brought on by their feafonable and proper ufe; but on the contrary, the laft will often fuddenly happen, where the body is fuffered to remain too long coftive, in confequence of the inteftines being over-diftended with indurated fœces, which create pain, and ftimulate them to frequent expulfion.

Head-ache, dilirium, or fever, are fometimes brought on by omitting the ufe
of

of laxatives, which may be given with safety at any time, but are indifpenfably neceffary about the fecond or third day after delivery ; efpecially in ftrong habits, where the patient does not intend to fuckle her child. In fhort, when the body is kept cool and temperate, by a *folutive regimen*, the better chance fhe will have to avoid fever, and the more regularly will all the natural fecretions and excretions be carried on.

The following laxative mixture, which is extremely gentle and pleafant, may be directed in the quantity of two or three fpoonful, or more, every two or three hours, till it produces its proper effect.

℞.

Ol. Ricini, cum Vitel. Ovi folut. ℥ i
Mann. calab. ℥ fs..
Aq. Hyffop. ℥ vi *fiat. Miftura.*

As foon as the bowels are fufficiently emptied, the following *antimonial powder* may immediately be adminiftered ;

stered, but sometimes it proves violently irritating, even in very small quantities, and will produce a dangerous superpurgation if not managed with the greatest caution; if this should happen, five drops of *thebaic tincture* may be occasionally added to each dose of the julep in which it is to be given.

R.

    Tart. emet. grifs

    Magnes. alb. ℨ *i*

accurate contere et fiat pulv. in sex portiones dividendus, quarum sumat unam 4ta. quaq. hora, vel subinde pro re nata, cum Cyath. Julep. sequentis.

R.

    Julep. e Camphor. ℥ *vii*

    Aq. Cin. spt. ℥ *ss. misce et fiat*

    Julepum ut supra exhibend.

When the first or second dose of powder produces no sensible effect, it ought to be given oftener, and in a larger quantity, 'till it either creates *nausea or gentle perspiration;*

perfpiration, without which, it feldom procures lafting relief. They fhould then be given by longer intervals, otherwife they will
be apt to weaken the patient ; however
upon the whole, I know nothing better
than *emetic tartar* in very fmall dofes, with
the addition of an *opiate*, if neceffary,
particularly after profufe evacuations ; for
it not only feems to combat the fever, but
much more fafely and effectually reftrains
the diarrhæa than aftringents ; by promo-
ting perfpiration and exciting naufea at the
ftomach, which, in fome meafure, *in-
verts* the exceffive periftaltic motion of the
inteftines, and prevents their frequent difcharge.

When the patient was much reduced by
returns of the evening paroxyfm, attended
with chilnefs, wandering pains, dejection of
fpirits, torpor and coldnefs of the extremities ; the third part of a grain of *emetic tartar*,
given about an hour before its approach, afforded fenfible relief, by producing a gentle
fweat. This

This fort of perfpiration may be moderately encouraged by plentiful dilution with weak tea ; or if the purging is violent, with rice-water, which generally agreed better with the patient than any thing elfe : But the fweats excited by heating regimen, which ftimulates the folids, and increafes their action on the blood, are highly prejudicial, and often deftructive to the patient, as well as thofe brought on by immoderate quantities of bed cloaths, or keeping the room too hot and clofe : For if thofe in perfect health foon grow faint and languid, when deprived of frefh, pure air ; the fame effect in a much greater degree, will necef-farily happen in the body, when weakened and oppreffed by the prefence of a difeafe.

Whenever the weather is intemperately hot, frefh air fhould always be allowed to breathe in at that part of the bedchamber moft diftant from the patient ;
which

which will gradually diffuse itself around, and revive her exceedingly, without the least danger of catching cold.

When the bowels are stripped of their mucus, they become so exceedingly tender, and the stools are so frequent, that she will sink under the discharge, if medicines of the irritating kind are any longer continued. Rice-water, used for common drink, may now be given with the addition of *gum arabic*, in the proportion of an ounce to a quart; and where the pulse is feeble and the patient much exhausted, a common spoonful of brandy may occasionally be added to that quantity, rather than wine, which is apt to turn sour on the stomach, and occasion eructation and pinchings in the bowels, with increase of the diarrhœa.

Nourishment that is light and simple should now be given often, in small quantities: Beef or chicken-water, poured from the dregs, after the fat has been taken off

the

the furface, and gently boiled with ground rice, and the addition of cinnamon, was found to agree with the ftomach, and is extremely foft and friendly to the bowels, as it will fupply them with artificial mucus, and nourifh the body at the fame time.

Whenever the ftrength is evidently perceived to fink under excefs of the diarrhœa; three grains of the *pil. e. ftyrace*, or the following bolus may be given at difcretion, with a fpoonful of cinnamonwater, or a very fmall quantity of any other grateful fluid. In fuch cafes, I obferved, that medicines in a folid form, were longeft retained, and thereforeare moft elegible.

℞.

> *Pulv. e Bolo comp. cum Opio ℈ſ*
> *Syr. e Core Aurant. q. s. ut fiat Bolus.*

Should the difcharge notwithftanding continue obftinate, with fevere pains in the bowels; clyfters, prepared with jelly of ftarch and the yolks of frefh eggs, in

equal

equal proportions, and diffolved in a sufficient quantity of rice-water, with thirty or
forty drops of *thebaic tincture* may be adminiftered by intervals, as occafion requires,
and will often procure immediate eafe.

The progrefs of this difeafe is frequently fo rapid, that there is not fufficient time to wait for a diftinct intermiffion, as in other fevers ; and therefore
if the *bark* is given at all, that muft be done
without heffitation, at the very firft favorable opportunity.

It was obferved, that this difeafe becomes
a true *febris purulenta* in its decline, from the
abforption of corrupted fluids ftagnating in
the cavity of the abdomen, altho' it was
ftrictly inflammatory in the beginning ; fo that
the *putrefaction* at that time exifting in
the habit, like the fizinefs of blood,
bilious vomiting, and diarrhæa, is truely
fymptomatic, being manifeftly the confequence and not the caufe of this fever.

Indeed,

Indeed, there is reason to believe that very few diseases are putrid in the beginning ; and that all, or most of them, have a tendency to become so towards their conclusion ; when the vital powers of the body are diminished, and its juices vitiated by preceding excess, or present defect of their natural motion.

Here it were to be wished, the efficacy of that soverign remedy, *Peruvian Bark,* might secure the patient from danger ; but both reason and experience, as well as the very nature of the disease itself, in a manner exclude hopes of relief ; for, altho' its liberal use might possibly be sufficient to destroy the putrefactive tendency begun in the body, by the absorption of corrupted fluids ; yet the large quantity still remaining in the abdomen, from which it cannot be evacuated, must necessarily prove destructive ; However, as we cannot always be certain when matter is formed, all possible means should be

K   tried

tried to prevent it ; and the bark ought to be given at all events, in large dofes often repeated.

It has been feared, the ufe of this medicine might fupprefs the *lochia* ; but I am affured from repeated experience, it may be given to women after delivery, with the greateft fafety whenever neceffary ; for, I never could obferve it produced any bad effect, or diminifhed that difcharge ; but on the contrary, often altered its quality for the better ; and alfo, rather feemed to increafe its quantity, efpecially in weak and delicate women, where the circulation was languid.

Sometimes the bark increafed the purging, and even brought it on again after it had ceafed ; in fuch cafes I found it neceffary to join five grains of pulv. e bolo comp. cum opio, with each of the following draughts.

R. Cort.

℞.

Cort. Peruv. pulv. ℥ *i*

Aq. font. lbifs leni igne coq. ad demid. & fub finem adjice.

Fol. Rofar. rub. ficc. ʒ *ii, cola.*

℞

Hujus colat. ℥ *ifs*

Extract. peruv. Cort. moll. ∋ *i*

Tinct. Cinn. ʒ *ij*

Confect. Alkerm. ʒ *i. fiat hauftus alternis horis exhibendus.*

When the firft draught was found to purge too much, I fometimes directed the following:

℞.

Cort. Peruv. ℥ *i*

Granat. ʒ *iii*

Aq. lbii ad demid. coq. & cola.

℞.

Colat. ℥ *ifs*

Tinct. Cinn. ʒ *ii*

—— *Thebaic* gtt. *v.*

Confect. Alkerm. ʒ *i f. hauftus.*

Blifters

Blisters have seldom been applied in the cases of lying-in women, on account of their severity, especially from the fear of that tormenting complaint the *strangury* ; but if, as many imagine, they produce their good effects by powerful stimulus, and raising inflammation on the skin, rather than the discharge they occasion ; the application of *sinapisms* would then effectually answer the purpose, without any danger of that disorder ; and therefore, will deserve the preference to *blisters* prepared with *cantharides* ; tho' I have not yet seen them sufficiently tried to speak from my own experience.

Notwithstanding, we are told blisters are improper and injurious, till the fulness and frequency of the pulse subsides ; I would wish it ever to be remembered, that whether we endeavour to relieve the patient by this or any other means, it must be *early*, or it will not be at all ; and therefore, after bleeding and evacuations, before that alarming symptom appears, which denotes *inflamma-*

tion

tion of the *omentum*, viz. pain darting downwards from the ftomach to the navel; it will be advifeable ·to apply a blifter or finapifm to one or both fides of the abdomen.

This practice, I think, will be fuffi-ciently juftified by the great relief they afford in fixed pleuritic pains, or where-ever there is local inflammation.

Volatile liniments, and penetrating topics, fuch as the following, have alfo been found ferviceable, particularly where the ufe of blifters appears exceptionable.

, ℞.

> *Ol. dulc. Amygd.* ℥ *ifs*
> *Camphor.* ℨ*fs.*
> *Spt. volat. aromat.* ℨ *iii mifce.*

Thefe are the beft reafons I am able to affign for the expediency of the reme-dies pointed out in the *Child-Bed Fever;* but I did not venture to truft to them from theory, nor expected that others fhould do fo, till obfervation and experience had

convinced

convinced me of their good effects ; particularly *early and copious bleeding*, and the
antiphlogiftic method which I am, therefore,
defirous to recommend, in preference to
every thing I have hitherto feen tried,
for the relief or cure of that fatal difeafe.

SECTION

SECTION III.

*Of the Prophylactic Method, ar Means con-
tributing to prevent the Difeafe.*

THE Child-bed Fever, when produced
by a diftemperature of air, like
the epidemic dyfentery, or ulcerous fore
throat, may at laft become infectious;
but when it only arifes from fuch accidental caufes as have already been enumerated, and which are confined to particular habits and conftitutions; I believe it
will then never communicate itfelf to a
fecond perfon.

It is probable, that many difeafes which
are forefeen, might either be prevented or
rendered lefs dangerous in their event, by
what is called the *prophylactic method,* a
branch of phyfic not hitherto fufficiently
cultivated or attended to.

K 4

Sydenham

Sydenham fuppofes, that of thofe women who fail in Child-bed, fcarcely one in ten of them die for want of ftrength, or by what they have endured in labor; but in confequence of their rifing too foon from bed; and therefore, he would not have them taken up at leaft till the tenth day after delivery. There is fo much reafon in this obfervation, that it ought to be duly regarded; but I think it may be faid with truth, that the proportion of thofe dying of Child-bed Fever, compared to the number who die from dangerous or diffi-cult labours, is at leaft double of that mentioned by Dr. *Sydenham.*

It is fometimes eafier to avoid the ap-proach of an evil than to find a remedy for it when prefent; therefore every attempt towards it will be more or lefs neceffary, in proportion to the danger of the evil itfelf; and fince it appears that Child-bed Fever, in the epidemic feafon, is fre-quently fatal; it would be a moft de-firable

firable circumftance, and a thing of real importance, if means could be devifed to fecure women from its malignant influence.

I am inclined to hope that this is poffible, at leaft in a certain degree; and the rather from what has been judicioufly and experimentally laid down on the fubject of *Fevers* and *Infection* by Dr. *Lind*; or, although the difeafe fhould appear, the fymptoms would probably be milder, and the event more favorable.

We have obferved, that when the body is endowed with exquifite fenfibility, the more it becomes difpofed to receive infection; would it not therefore be rational and expedient, when this difeafe is moft frequent and fatal, to adminifter fuch medicines, *a few days before and after delivery*, as have been known to ftrengthen the conftitution, and diminifh the fenfibility and irritability of the habit ? If fo, nothing would fo powerfully contribute to this end, as the liberal ufe of *Peruvian Bark,*

with

with the calybeate waters, particularly those of *Pyrmont* or *Spa*. Where the nervous fystem is extremely delicate, and thrown into diforder from flight accidental caufes; the prudent ufe of *opium* will alfo be attended with great advantage; it will reftore reft to the body, and tranquility to the mind, by difpoffeffing it of thofe difquieting ideas which difturb and pervert the natural fecretions, and tend to excite fever. It has been fuppofed, this medicine will fufpend the bodily powers, and render them torpid or fluggifh in fhaking off difeafes, but this appears too hafty a conjecture; for in women of hyfteric habits, who fuffer from agitation of mind, or want of fleep, and where the pulfe from thence becomes quick, weak and tremulous; there is not perhaps to be found, a more fovereign and effectual cordial in the whole Materia Medica.

It

It will alfo be neceffary to caution the patient againft all fuch adventitious caufes as have been known fingly to produce this fever, or to add influence to the atmofphere in bringing it on; fuch as fudden terror, or long-continued diftrefs of mind; rifing too foon from bed after delivery; errors in diet; or cold air admitted to the body in a full ftream. Her food fhould be fimple, eafy of digeftion, and chiefly of the vegetable acefcent kind; her drink may be wine and water, acidulated with orange-juice, or any of the grateful acids. She fhould ufe gentle exercife, and breathe a free open air, guarding againft all fudden changes from one extreme to another. The bed-chamber after delivery, fhould be cool, and neither incommoded with much noife or ftrong light. In a word, the body fhould be kept ftill and quiet, and every thing carefully avoided which difagreeably engages attention of mind.

Nothing

Nothing will fooner difpofe the fluids to putrefaction, than *long fafting* which occafions a ftinking breath, and loofenefs of the teeth ; fo that animals ftarved to death, may be faid in reality to rot alive. From this circumftance may be inferred, the great advantage of frequently taking aliment, or attemperating acefcent fluids, to prevent difeafes of the putrid kind ; for it has been obferved, they will furvive a long time by the ufe of water only, which carries off the acrimonious falts, and rancid oils, by urine ; and thereby hinders the juices from becoming putrid.

How far fome of thofe Rules and Cautions might be conducive to the prefervation of women, if duly regarded *before delivery*, I cannot from experience determine ; as the patients at the *Weftminfter Hofpital* were always received in actual labour; and confidering how much people in general are fwayed by opinion and vulgar prejudice ; I did not chufe to urge this matter

too

too far in private practice, left by its novelty, it should carry with it the appearance of an experiment, to which those of weak understandings are always averse, however safe and rational it might be in itself, or beneficial in the conclusion.

The pernicious custom of binding the body too tight, ought also to be avoided; as it will produce difficulty of breathing, head-ach, and oppression at stomach.

Particular odors will likewise occasion bad effects, and have an inconceivable power on some particular women of delicate hysterical habits; being sometimes known to bring on sickness at stomach, delirium or faintings.

I think it will be adviseable for the patient to suckle her child, at least for the first three weeks or a month, although the principal danger seems to be over before the end of a fortnight.

Nothing

Nothing will fo foon difpofe women to
this fever, as breathing a putrid, confined
air, efpecially if it be warm and moift ; for
thefe qualities deftroy its elaftic power,
and not only render it unfit for refpiration,
but alfo more apt to generate difeafes of
the putrid kind.

Peu gives a very ftriking and felf-evident
proof of the truth of this affertion ; having obferved, in hofpitals where women
were delivered in wards among the
wounded, many of them died ; fo as to
occafion a fufpicion of the fkill or attention
of thofe who delivered them.* The matter being properly confidered, they difcovered, that this uncommon mortality was
owing to the *putrid effluvia* continually
exhaling from the wounds of the fick ;
and as a confirmation of this conjecture, it
was obferved, that when the number of
wounded

* *Peu* la Pratiq. des accouch. liv. ii. chap. i. pag. 268.

wounded patients increafed, fo did this contagious fever among child-bed women, and vice verfa.

This circumftance will fuggeft a ufeful hint, which ought to be duly regarded by all thofe who have the direction and fuperintendance of public *Lying-in Hofpitals*. The wards fhould not be over crowded with beds, in order to avoid the danger of breathing air rendered impure by too great a number of people confined in a narrow fpace ; and alfo the cries of children and noife of fuch women as may happen to be in labor. The different wards fhould not only be kept exceeding clean, but alfo ventilated by a ftream of frefh air paffing through them, as they become empty by fucceffion.

When the heat of weather is extreme ; the air may be rendered cool and refrefhing, as well as antifeptic, by fprinkling the boards with pure water, and vinegar ; for all fluids in a ftate of evaporation, have been found to generate cold.

This

This method was conftantly obferved at the *Weftminfter-lying-in Hofpital,* during the epidemic feafon. Such wards may alfo be fumigated with fragrant gums, as thofe of *Myrrh,* and *gum copal,* with the addition of *Cafcarilla bark* ; but above all the fteams of boiling vinegar, to which *lavendar flowers* have been added, with a fufficient quantity of *camphire,* may frequently be taken into the lungs, as the moft grateful and effectual prefervative that perhaps is to be found.

That excellent practical author, Dr. *Lind* obferves, the admiffion of pure air, or the moft perfect ventilation, is not always fufficient to diflodge the *infectious matter* from the place of its refidence ; he therefore recommends the application of *fire* and *fmoke,* as the moft certain and effectual means of extinguifhing the fource of contagion : He alfo advifes the burning of wood fires, for, it has been experimentally found, that the fmoke of burning wood

not

not only tends greatly to abate its violence, but also to preserve the uninfected from its malignant power.

He directs the wards, or infected chambers of the sick, to be closely shut up, and then fumigated with *brimstone strewed on charcoal fires*; he further adds, that except the *plague* itself, no infection more pestilental and mortal has been known to prevail any where, than those in some ships; yet he never heard of any ship which did not immediately become healthy, after being thus carefully and properly fumigated; and if we are not misinformed, some very late accounts from abroad assure us, that the *plague* itself was prevented by methods of the like kind.

In the year 1775, when the Child-Bed Fever again prevailed with great violence, at the Westminster-Lying-In Hospital, and proved fatal to several women; I directed the beds in the wards to be taken down, the curtains to be washed, and bed-

L   cloath

cloaths placed in the fun, in a ftream of frefh air : The wards being then clofely fhut up, were fumigated for two days with *Sulphur*, *Pitch*, and *Tobacco Stalks* ftrewed on charcoal fires ; after which the walls were white-wafh'd, and the wards being thoroughly cleaned, were fprinkled with *camphorated vinegar*. The beds being then replaced, fuch was the falutary effects of this method, in putting a ftop to the difeafe, that of feveral patients foon after admitted, only two were feized with it, one of which died.

Next to the fmoke of burning wood, efpecially *fpruce*, or that of the teribinthinate kind ; he efteems the fumes of gunpowder, for purifying a tainted air. All bodies, during their confumption by fire, afford a large quantity of *mephitic air*, which has been found powerfully to refift putrefaction ; and upon this principle, I believe, the good effect of the preceding method folely depends.

Experi-

Experiments fhew, that animals cannot long furvive, nor flame fubfift, without the acceffion of frefh air ; even a common candle will require a gallon of this fluid in a minute. Confidering therefore, that the atmofphere is continually injured by the corruption of perifhable bodies, and the effect of artificial fires, with thofe natural, and more immenfe ones, proceeding from volcanos ; it feemed a matter of wonder, how the air could ftill preferve its original purity ; 'till Dr. *Priefly* difcovered, that the perfpirable matter or *effluvia of vegetables* is the grand refource, and fovereign remedy which nature applies to reftore the falutary principles of air, thus injured and rendered unfit for refpiration.

From this circumftance, it will appear no irrational caution, to place pots of myrtle, fouthern-wood, or mint in the chamber of the fick, during the *epidemical feafon* ; as thofe vegetables are continually throwing off their *antifeptic vapor.* But it is to be

L 2

observed

observed, that the good thus produced is not owing to any aromatic quality ; for vegetables of an offensive smell, and even such as were almost inodorous, were found most powerful in resisting the putrescent quality of air.

Hence the custom, with some of putting green boughs round the sick, or sprinkling the ground with new gathered leaves, and flowers, on the supposition of affording refreshment, and disposing the patient to sleep, does not seem ill-founded ; for although they were ignorant how such relief was procured, they might, notwithstanding, have sagacity enough to observe the effect was certain.

The *Matrons* of all *Public Hospitals,* in cases of extreme danger, ought to administer the medicines prescribed with their own hands; they should also take care the *nurses* do their duty, and frequently supply the patients with clean, well-aired linen ; otherwise, the warmth of weather in summer, added

to

to the heat of body, may occasion a corruption of the lochia, which will taint
the air, and not only render it offensive,
but highly noxious.

During the first week or ten days after
delivery, women should wear half shifts and
skirts, for the greater convenience of
changing them with ease, as occasion may
require.

In such *Hospitals* there ought to be particular beds or couches, for the sake of delicacy and neatness, as well as to keep the
rest dry and clean : These delivery-beds, as
they are called, being placed upon casters,
may be brought close to another bed prepared
for the reception of the patient, into which
she may be gently conveyed, after resting a
little to recover her strength and spirits
from the fatigue of labor : This method
will afford exceeding comfort and refreshment to a woman after delivery, and will

L 3

also

alfo contribute greatly to her recovery, by removing her from the wet linen, which otherwife, would fubject her to take cold.

The mattreffes and bedding fhould often be infpected, and frequently expofed to the fun and open air ; and all foul linen fhould immediately be removed out of the wards ; together with the putrid, bilious fluids, rejected by the ftomach or bowels.

When the patients at the *Weftminfter Lying-In Hofpital* were helplefs, and unable to fit up in bed to take refrefhment ; they were fupported by a kind of *half chair*, made for that purpofe, and placed behind their backs, which was found extremely ufeful on fuch occafions.

SECTION

SECTION IV.

History and Treatment of the Child-Bed Fever further illustrated by Cases, with Practical Remarks on the whole. Also occasional Animadversions on the Section *of the* Pubes, *as a substitute for the* Cæsarian Operation.

THE reader will find that the following Cases were not set down with any intention to shew how successfully they were treated ; but rather as examples of the dangerous tendency of this disease, which was oftentimes such as neither art or nature had power to subdue : I have paid no regard to the caution of omitting some of those where it was fatal, or of inserting others when the event was favorable ; in short, I have no where put a mask on the face of the disease, or suppressed the mention of a single circumstance whic h I thought could prove of the least use in

L 4

being

being known ; but have, at all events, defcribed it as I found it in the *epidemical feafon*, and as it will be found by others, under the like circumftances, viz. danger- ous in its nature, and difficult of cure.

From what has been advanced, it appears that the human body is fo conftructed, as only to fuftain violence to a certain degree ; and therefore, if the force of a dangerous difeafe be fuperadded to that indifpofition brought on the habit by delivery, it is gene- rally then much more fatal than at any other time ; fo that certain maladies which might have been feparately endured, be- come deftructive by their united power. In the *fmall pox*, for inftance, taken in the natural way, about one in feven or eight may probably die ; but fuppofing thofe affected with it to be women at the *point of delivery*, very few of the whole number will be found to recover.

C A S E

CASE I.

Elizabeth Waters, a young woman of a strong healthy habit, aged twenty one, was delivered in the *Weftminfter New Lying-In Hofpital*, *April* the 7th, 1768. On the fourth day after, fhe complained of head-ach, which fhe faid was owing to her being difturbed by another patient in labour, who lay near her in the fame ward : her pulfe was tolerably good, and neither very full nor frequent, but as her head-ach continued till the next morning ; eight ounces of blood were then taken from the arm, which afforded her much relief. She had milk in her breafts, and the *lochia* were difcharged in due quantity, without any pain or tenfion of the belly. Two days after, the pain in her head returned with violence, attended with thirft and fever, for which fhe loft feven ounces more blood : fhe took a laxative mixture, which had its proper effect, and afterwards the faline draughts

draughts every four or five hours, from which she seemed better ; but as the pain in her head still continued, I directed *leeches* to her temples the next evening, which gave her ease.

She was apparently much better for a few days, her appetite being good, and her aspect chearful ; but soon after relapsed, and was seized with severe and excruciating pains, like those of acute rheumatism, in her limbs and body : She became quite helpless, and was not able to turn herself in bed without assistance.

I attended this patient with Dr. *Bricken-den*, one of the physicians of the Hospital. We directed antimonial powders, which she took as occasion required, but without much relief ; as the pains continued, with a slow, lingering fever, for seven or eight days ; and as they abated, were succeeded by a number of bluish discolorations on the skin, which were terminated by abscesses

in

in different parts of her body : As they advanced flowly, and did not point with tenfion and rednefs, but were foft and of a pale, livid hue ; we directed the *bark*, with wine and good nourifhment to quicken the circulation, and affift nature in bringing them forwards, as they plainly appeared of the critical kind ; but notwithftanding they were conftantly poulticed twice a-day, not one of them came to fuppuration fo as to break, even at the end of fix weeks from the beginning of the diforder ; fhe was therefore removed to the *Weftminfter Hofpital,* where the abfceffes, in number *eighteen,* as I was informed, were opened, and after remaining fome weeks there, fhe at laft recovered ; and being cured and difcharged, came and returned thanks at the *Lying-in-Hofpital.*

C A S E.

CASE II.

Elizabeth Becket, aged twenty-six, and of a healthy conftitution, after a difficult labor which lafted feveral hours, was delivered of a dead child at the *Hofpital, February* the 18th, 1769.

She was affected with head-ach, and fick at ftomach, from the day of delivery, but did not vomit.

February 19. Her pulfe being frequent, and fomewhat full and ftrong, and the head-ach violent, I directed eight ounces of blood to be taken away; an emollient clyfter was then adminiftered, and fhe afterwards took the faline draughts, with *fperm. ceti* every five or fix hours. Towards evening fhe had four bilious ftools, and appeared better.

20th. Her thirft was exceffive, her tongue white and dry, fhe perfpired little, and had three evacuations by ftool; fhe
diluted

diluted plentifully with weak tea, and took her medicines as before.

21ft. Slept little, her eyes were blood-fhot and prominent, and her head-ach not abated ; her fkin was dry, and her pulfe being ftronger than ufual in fuch cafes, eight ounces more blood were taken away.

22d. She flept the preceding night ; her head-ach greatly relieved, and all the febrile fymptoms manifeftly abated ; notwithftanding, fhe remained weak and helplefs, and had involuntary ftools for a few days after ; but as her fteength increafed, this inconvenience went off, and in a fortnight's time from the firft attack, fhe perfectly recovered.

The *milk* continued till the fifth day, and the *lochial difcharge* did not feem altered from its natural ftate.

REMARKS.

I would not here have it inferred that thefe two patients recovered becaufe bleeding

ing was directed ; but rather from their having this fever when the season was not *epidemical* ; for I have already remarked, that the attack is not then so violent, and all the subsequent symptoms are less severe : The shivering fit in the beginning is generally less, and the diarrhœa and bilious vomiting are either inconsiderable, or do not appear at all ; the pulse is neither so quick or weak, and the disease, instead of being terminated about the tenth or eleventh day, is often protracted beyond that period, from *acute* becoming *truly chronical*, and then seldom proving fatal.

Eliz. Burges was the first patient seized with *Child-Bed Fever* in the epidemic season ; she was delivered on the 6th of *December*, 1769, and died about twelve days after ; but the particulars of her case I cannot distinctly remember.

C A S E III.

Juliana Thompson, aged twenty-one, and of a delicate habit, having received a stroke

on

on her belly, was fuddenly feized with labor, and delivered in a chair as fhe was coming to the hofpital, *December* the 7th, 1769.

She continued pretty well for the two firft days, but was rather languid and dejected in fpirits, having had a flight uterine hæmorrhage from the time fhe re-received the hurt to that of being delivered.

December 10. Was feverifh and thirfty, and complained of great pain in her head; there was no appearance of *milk*, and the *lochia* where difcharged in natural quantity. She took lenitive elect. with oil of almonds, which procured her two or three evacuations; thirft and fever were abated, and her head-ach was much better.

11. Continued better, and was able to fit up in bed.

12th. Her face was florid, her cheeks were befet with a deep crimfon color, and her pulfe was quick and weak; the tongue looked

looked clean, though her thirſt was intenſe; ſhe diluted plentifully with tea and barley-water; the ſaline mixture with ſperm. ceti was given occaſionally, and a clyſter of beef-water directed to be adminiſtered. Towards evening, difficulty of breathing came on, with oppreſſion at her breaſt, and pain in her left ſide.

When I viſited this patient with Dr. *Ford*, we directed the *tartar emetic* in the third part of a grain to be given every four or five hours, and a *bliſter* to be applied to her ſide; the emollient clyſter was alſo repeated.

She had ſix or ſeven motions in the night, and the next day appeared eaſier, but was languid and weak; her pulſe continued very quick, and the bliſter did not riſe.

As there was ſediment in her urine, with ſigns of remiſſion, we though it adviſeable to try the *bark* in decoction; but it purged her immoderately, although the

ſimple

simple cinnamon-water was added, and therefore it was left off.

Next day she complained of pains shooting downwards from her stomach to the navel, for which *a volatile liniment* was applied, but as it did not procure much relief; we directed a *warm bath* the day following, in the manner already mentioned at p. 119 ; a long flannel gown being next her skin, she was afterwards put into a warm bed, and supplied with beef-tea and other fluids, in order to encourage perspiration.

Bladders half filled with warm water, and wrapped in flannels, were applied to her stomach and sides, where she still complained of pain and oppression, and the emollient clysters were also continued, with g^{tt}. xxx of *thebaic tincture*.

The next day her belly began to swell, though the purging still continued ; she had partial, faint sweats on her breast and face, and was now extremely weak, though

M perfectly

perfectly fenfible, but could take nothing except nourifhment for feveral days before her death, which happened on the 25th of *December*; being the fifteenth day from the time of the febrile attack.

Margaret Walker, another patient in the fame ward, was delivered on the 11th of *December*, and fickened foon after the former: They both lay ill at the fame time, and labored under fymptoms fo exactly fimilar, that it would be unneceffary to fet down the particulars of this laft cafe: She died on the 21ft of the faid month, nine days after being feized with the difeafe.

CASE IV.

Mrs. Y. a lady near the *Abbey* in *Weftminfter*; young, and of a ftrong and healthy habit, after a labor perfectly natural, was fuddenly attacked with a violent fhivering fit, the third day after delivery, being the 1ft of *January* 1770: She

She was also affected with a thrilling, uncommon sensation, as if a cold, wet sheet had been wrapped round her body.

She complained of head-ach, and was sick at stomach ; during the excess of febrile heat, her pulse beat a hundred and thirty strokes in a minute, and was more full and strong than usual in this fever ; her countenance was florid, and much altered from its natural state, having an unusual stare with her eyes.

Small portions of *emetic tartar*, viz. the fourth part of a grain, were given with the saline mixture, every four hours : She diluted plentifully with barley water and balm-tea, but did not perspire.

Second day after the attack, a violent bilious purging came on ; the antimonial powders were then given by longer intervals ; the saline mixture was discontinued, and emollient clysters were directed : She took rice-water, and the white decoction for common drink.

M 2   The

The fever and diarrhœa continued violent for three or four days; her belly
fwelled, and fhe frequently complained
of much pain at the bottom of her ftomach, and towards the navel: Sometimes
there feemed to be obfcure figns of remiffion in the morning; but towards
evening, the fever again returned with
violence.

As fhe apparently grew worfe, and as I
was, at that time, ill and unable to give
her due attendance, I defired Dr. *Hunter*
might be called in, which was accordingly done. He directed eight ounces of
blood to be taken away; the clyfters to
be repeated, and a bladder, filled with
fcalded bran, to be applied warm to the
umbilical region. The next day, I met
Dr. *Hunter* and Dr. *Hugh Smith*: The faline draughts, with ʒ fs of *confect. damocratis*, were directed every fix hours,
and in other refpects, much the fame
method was purfued as before.

When

When Dr. *Smith* vifited this patient with me the day following, we found her delirious, and therefore, inftead of the confect. damocratis, Ә i of the *pulv. contrayer. c.* was added to each faline draught, which was ordered to be continued as before : Four fpoonful of *tincture* of *rofes* were given by intervals and clyfters of chicken-water directed to be adminiftered frequently. The two following days I was prevented from feeing her ; during which, fhe took medicines of the warm cordial kind, but without perfpiration, or any abatement of the febrile fymptoms.

A few days before her death, fhe was delirious ; her eyes were blood-fhot and filled with involuntary tears ; a *miliary eruption* appeared very thick on her breaft and body, and her ftools, which were frequent and very fœtid, came away infenfibly.

M 3   *Leeches*

Leeches were then applied to her temples; the clyfters were repeated, and her ftrength was fupported by nourifhment and wine, but all without a falutary effect; for on the twelfth of *January* fhe died; and feveral hours before her death became perfectly fenfible.

The *lochia* were difcharged iu due quantity, but there was no fecretion of *milk.*

REMARKS.

The figns of putrefaction in this patient before death, were very evident: The fmell of the room feveral days after fhe was buried being intolerably offenfive, notwithftanding it had been thoroughly cleanfed and fumigated with frankincenfe.

Purgative medicines, which are found fo extremely beneficial in the fecondary, putrid fever after the fmall-pox, cannot here be employed to advantage, becaufe of the tendernefs of the bowels and exceffive lofs of ftrength from the preceding diarrhæa;

fo

fo that *Peruvian bark*, with *opiates* and frequent nourifhment, feem moft likely to afford relief, where that is in the power of medicine ; but unfortunately, the ftate of the patient is generally at this time fuch, for the reafons already given, as excludes all human affiftance.

Where the ftools are exceffively putrid, it might be worth while to try the effects of fluids which contain a large quantity of fixed air, given in clyfters, as they have been found powerfully to refift putrefaction, agreeable to fome late hints in Dr. *Prieftly*'s curious tract on the method of impregnating water with fixed air.

Elizabeth Tomkins, alfo died of this fever, the 15th of *January*, 1770.

C A S E V.

Mary Evans, aged twenty-nine, was delivered *February* the 5th, 1770, without any uncommon circumftance attending her labor, which was eafy and natural.

M 4   Her

Her habit of body was apparently good, but being crooked and narrow-chefted, fhe was fubject to habitual difficulty of breathing. She took an anodyne draught, with fperm. ceti, and paffed a good night after delivery.

February the 6th. Perfpired gently, and was free from pain and fever.

7th. At feven in the morning attacked with a flight fhivering fit which lafted about fifteen minutes, but was not fucceeded by any violent-degree of feverifh heat; fhe took the antimonial powders every three or four hours, and fell into a gentle perfpiration, which feemed to relieve her; an emollient clyfter was alfo directed.

8th. Refted the preceding night, and continued tolerably eafy; fhe had one bilious ftool in the morning, was weak and languid, but free from pain and got fome fleep.

9th.

9th. At nine, in the morning had a shivering fit, which was relieved by drinking warm fluids and the application of hot flannels to her extremities and sides; in a few hours the cold fit in a flight degree returned, and was succeeded by fever, and partial sweats on her breast and temples; she had some rest the former part of the night, but at two o'clock was waked by violent *gripings* and *tormina* in the bowels, followed by nine or ten bilious stools, after which she had ease.

10th. About twelve at noon was seized with great difficulty of breathing, and in the time of inspiration, affected with intolerable acute pain striking down from her breast to the navel; but there was no tension or pain in the belly, nor any symptom that could strictly be called uterine, the *lochia being neither fœtid or deficient in quantity:* her pulse at the same time was quick, and unequal; but considering her great difficulty of breathing, fix ounces of blood were

were taken away, and the following mixture was given occasionally ; a broth clyster with g^{tt.} xx. of thebaic tincture, was also directed, and she took rice-water or decoct. alb. for common drink.

℞.

> *Lact. Ammoniac.* ℥ *vii.*
> *Sperm. Ceti folut.* ℥ *ii.*
> *Elix. paregoric.* ℥ *iii.*

Fiat Miftura cujus fumat Cochleari a duo fubinde urgente dolore vel dyfpnœa.

After bleeding, her pulfe became somewhat ftronger, and its ftrokes were more diftinct and free ; the pain and difficulty of breathing were a little abated, and fhe paffed a tolerable good night with refrefhing flumbers.

11th. In the morning fhe was weak, but free from pain or much fever, and breathed with confiderable eafe ; about three in the afternoon, fhe became feverifh again ; and in the evening, her pulfe was quick and almoft imperceptibly weak ; her

her limbs were cold, and partial, clammy fweats overfpread her face and temples.

I directed two fpoonful of the following mixture to be given every two or three hours :

R.

Spec. e. Scord. c. cum Opio ʒ *i*

Aq. Cin. fimp, ʒ *vi*

—*Nucis Mofehat.* ʒ *i*

Syr. e Cort. aurant. ʒ *fs fiat Miftura.*

An anodyne clyfter was directed as before : her extremities were kept warm with hot flannels, and fhe paffed a reftlefs night, being delirious by turns. At four in the morning, fhe had four black, foetid ftools, which were voided without pain. At feven, fhe was perfectly fenfible, and fo continued 'till the hour of ten, at which time fhe calmly expired, being the fifth day from the febrile commencement.

The *locbial difcharge* was natural, and fhe had milk at the ufual time, which left her foon after the febrile attack.

DISSECTION.

DISSECTION.

After making an incision into the abdomen, from the navel to each anterior angle of the os ilium, and turning down the muscular flap over the pubes ; several ounces of *white, curd-like pus* covered the surface of the inteftines ; it did not run out when the abdominal cavity was laid open, being of a much thicker confiftence than common matter. On further examination, I found the greateft part of the *omentum* melted down, and formed this *purulent concrete* ; and that the fmall portion remaining, was much inflamed, and flightly adhered to the inteftines. About a pint and a half of putrid fluid, like whey, was found in the cavity of the pelvis, mixed with concreted matter, and bits of black, grumous blood which feemed to have efcaped from the eroded veffels of the *omentum*.

The

The *uterus* was contracted to the size of a swan's egg, and shrunk down below the brim of the pelvis: On cutting into its cavity, small flaky pieces of the false chorion were found adhering to its surface, but it did not contain any kind of fluid; in short, this part, as well as the bladder, was perfectly sound, and without the least mark of inflammation, or any other morbid affection.

The substance of the *liver* was also sound, but appeared pale, bloodless, and as if it had been par-boiled; the gall-bladder was full of blackish bile.

The *stomach* and *intestines* were in their natural state; the first contained half a pint of a watery blackish fluid, which smelled like rancid bile; and in the last was found twice that quantity of dark green fluid, somewhat like that in the stomach.

The *spleen* was large but sound.

The

The sternum being raised, the lungs appeared of a livid hue, but on cutting into their substance, neither pus nor tubercles were found, nor any signs of inflammation; only the left lobe, at its posterior and superior part, slightly adhered to the pleura.

The veins on the neck and breast, on the left side, were enlarged to three times their natural diameter, and filled with blood of a bluish color.

REMARKS.

When respiration becomes extremely difficult and painful, in diseases of the thorax or abdomen, especially those of the inflammatory kind, nothing affords such speedy relief as bleeding; for if the breath is drawn in with excessive pain, the lungs cannot be sufficiently inflated, and therefore the blood will not be freely discharged from the heart through the pulmonary artery; hence

hence great oppreffion and anxiety at the præcordia, fo often complained of by the patient, which if not fpeedily removed, may produce a mortal fuffocation ; but when *matter* is already unluckily formed, as in the preceding cafe, it will then plainly appear, that the patient is paft the affiftance of art, and that neither bleeding or any thing elfe can avail.

As this difeafe is principally feated in the *omentum*, and uniformly produces inflammation of that part (*epiploitis*) I think it will ftrongly enforce a neceffity for the early lofs of blood, together with the immediate application of *blifters* to the fides, or even to the umbilical region, to prevent, if poffible, a morbid affection of the vifcera, which when once begun, is rapid in its progrefs, and generally fatal in the conclufion.

C A S E VI.

Ann Hewatfon, aged twenty-fix, and of a delicate habit, was delivered *February* the
5th,

5th, 1770. Her cafe was fomewhat laborious, and the child's birth fucceeded by a difcharge of grumous blood from the uterus ; the *placenta* came away without affiftance, about an hour after delivery ; fhe was eafy in the night, and had refrefhing fleep.

6th. Being inclined to fleep, took a fperm. ceti emulfion without any opiate ; perfpired gently, had a good night with natural reft, and waked free from pain or fever. The lochial difcharge was large in quantity and foetid ; but the belly was foft, and without pain.

7th. Continued eafy, and had a moderate fecretion of milk.

8th. About ten in the morning, after a breakfaft of tea, without any evident caufe, fhe was fuddenly attacked with *rigor*, which fhook her whole body like an ague fit ; the fhivering lafted above half an hour, gradually becoming lefs and lefs intenfe from its onfet.

She

She took the emetic draught already mentioned, which operated mildly towards evening, the antimonial powders were given by due intervals : fhe was extremely feverifh, thirfty, and reftlefs at night, but somewhat relieved by a free perfpiration, which came on about twelve o'clock.

9th. Had four bilious, frothy ftools, preceded by violent pains and gripings in the bowels : an emollient clyfter was injected. Her pulfe was quick and weak, and the febrile fymptoms violent. She had a very reftlefs night, but only one evacuation and without pain.

10th. In the morning had nine or ten blackifh ftools, mixed with mucus, which were extremely offenfive, and attended with great pain : her pulfe was exceffive quick, fhe breathed laborioufly, as it were by jerks, and complained of great oppreffion acrofs her breaft and ftomach, and of pain ftriking down under her fhoulder-blade, when fhe drew in her breath. Eight ounces

N of

of blood were taken away, and a ftarch clyfter with g^{tt}. xxx of tinct. thebaic. was adminiftered : fhe only now took rice-water, with a fmall portion of brandy in it, as every thing elfe purged her immoderately. Towards evening, feemed better, her pulfe not fo frequent, the pain and feverifh fymptoms were fomewhat abated.

11th. Hot and reftlefs, with faint fweats on her breaft, neck, and face. Emollient clyfter repeated, without the opiate ; after which fhe had fome fleep.

12th. The clyfter came away with a bilious ftool ; fhe was manifeftly much worfe, her pulfe being very quick, and thirft intenfe ; fhe breathed laborioufly, had a fixed crimfon color in her cheeks, and was alfo much troubled with a cough and vifcid phlegm, which fhe was unable to expectorate, but found relief by taking the following mixture :

℞. *Sal.*

R.

   Sal. Abfinth. ℥ *i*

   Succ. Limon. ℥ *ifs, peracta effervefcentia,* affund.

   Aq. Hyffop. ℥ *vi*

   Elix. paregoric ʒ *ii*

   Syr. balfamic. ʒ *iii*

   Fiat Miſtura cujus ſumat Cochlearia duo ſubinde pro re nata.

13th. She was fupported by a cordial julep when faint, with light nourifhment, and wine given by fpoonfuls.

14th. Breathed with great difficulty, her pulfe very quick and weak. She had partial fweats on her ftomach, breaft, and face, attended with coldnefs of the extremities, great langour, and all the fymptoms of approaching death : fhe died about two in the morning, being the eighth day after the attack.

REMARKS.

At the time of the fhivering fit, which happened on the third day ; this patient

had

had plenty of milk in her breasts, which afterwards suddenly disappeared, and was totally gone off in the evening; her breasts being then loose and empty: *the defect of milk is therefore manifestly a consequence of the morbid cause.*

There is however one circumstance, which, although it seems to controvert this opinion, I cannot help mentioning, viz. those who were seized with this fever, were not subject to abscesses of the breasts; and of those who happened to have such abscesses, I have never known one die; neither are they subject to diarrhœa, or much symptomatic fever, although the pain attending a suppuration of the breast, is often very acute.

The putrid discharge of *lochia* in this case, appears merely accidental, and only owing to a corruption of coagulated blood retained in the uterus, from the access of air, like that which came away soon after delivery.

Phœbe

Phœbe Hill, aged nineteen, was also violently seized with this fever on the eleventh of *February*, and contrary to my expectation, recovered, and was discharged in perfect health, on the 3d of *March*.

She was *blooded early and liberally*, and treated much like the former patient, but I did not take minutes of her case.

C A S E.   VII.

Elizabeth Gardner, aged thirty-two, was delivered in the Hospital the 11th of *February*, 1770; her labor was natural, and her habit of body strong and healthy, although she had been troubled with a violent cough for several weeks before delivery.

12th.   Her pulse was full and frequent, attended with great thirst, sickness at stomach, and pain in her head and bowels; she took saline mixture, with sperm. ceti, and an emollient clyster was administered: She also drank plentifully of

N 3   weak

weak tea and barley-water, but did not perfpire, and paffed the night without fleep.

13th. I vifited this patient with Dr. *Ford.* Her pulfe being exceeding quick, and more full and ftrong than ufual, attended with exceffive thirft, a violent head-ach, and dry fkin ; we directed ten ounces of blood immediately to be taken away : A lenitive electuary was afterwards given, and an emollient clyfter, which produced two or three lax motions : She diluted plentifully, but did not perfpire, and paffed a reftlefs night.

The fecretion of *milk* was moderate, and the *lochial difcharge* natural.

14th. In the morning had fome refrefhing fleep, with gentle perfpiration ; thirft and fever fomewhat abated : She had three evacuations by ftool, but ftill complained much of intolerable fhooting pain in her head, efpecially at the time

of

of coughing : Eight ounces more blood were taken away, which was not near so sizy as that first drawn.

15th. Much disturbed by her cough in the night, perspired little, and had no sleep, though her head-ach was somewhat better.

16th. In the evening, her pulse was extremely quick, thirst immoderate, and all the febrile symptoms increased : she was sick at stomach, and had three bilious stools, with severe gripings in her bowels. The *antimonial powders* were given every three or four hours ; about two hours after taking the second, she threw up a large quantity of viscid phlegm, mixed with bile, and in the night had eight or nine black stools, the last very fœtid, and mixed with blood and mucus. She was delirious by turns, very restless, and had partial, faint sweats on her breast and face.

The

The vitel. ovi, with mucilage of starch, was dissolved in rice-water, and injected as a clyster; and she took the following draught,

℞.

  Sperm. Ceti. Solut. ℥ *fs*
  Pulv. e Tragacanth. C. Ə *i*
  Aq. Cin. Simp. ℥ *ifs*
  Tinct. Thebaic. gtt. xv.
  Syr. e. Mecon. ℥ *i fiat haustus.*

17th. Her stomach and bowels were much relieved, she slept in the night and waked refreshed; her pulse was weak but equal, and she perspired moderately.

18th. Better in all respects, but complained of great soreness in her bowels at the time of coughing: She took the anodyne draught at night, and the starch clysters were continued with light nourishment.

19th. Weak, but continued easy, her pulse regular, and she perspired gently. Instead of medicines, she now took calf's-

            foot

foot-jelly, and nourifhing broth, to repair her ftrength.

20th. From this time gradually continued to recover, and the 9th of *March*, fhe was difcharged from the hofpital in perfect health.

Ann Williams, who was delivered in the hofpital on the 14th of February, was feized with this fever, and recovered under the *like treatment.*

Elizabeth Coufenitt, of a fickly, confumptive habit, alfo had the fever the 23d of *February*, and died the 3d of *March :* There was no fecretion of *milk*, but the *lochial difcharge* was natural. She was treated in the ufual manner, but *not blooded.*

CASE VIII.

Ann Simms, aged twenty-two, apparently healthy and ftrong, was delivered on *Tuefday* the 6th of *March* ; her cafe was fomewhat laborious, the child's head being

being large, and detained several hours within the bones of the pelvis · An emollient clyster was directed in the evening, and she took an anodyne draught ; passed a restless night, and without the least perspiration.

7th. Feverish and thirsty, pulse quick and somewhat full, and her skin dry. She took the saline mixture, and diluted plentifully with nitrous drink ; a clyster of beef-water was given in the evening ; had a very indifferent night, and little rest.

8th. A little better ; she had milk in her breasts, and being costive, complained of head-ach. A cathartic clyster was administered in the evening, which procured two evacuations, and her head was easier.

9th and 10th. Somewhat feverish, and restless, though free from pain.

11th. Continued very restless ; the pulse was quick, her tongue white and dry, and her thirst intense, without any perspiration:

fpiration : At night, fhe took a faline draught, with ten grains of *nitre* and gtt. xv. of *thebaic tincture*, but had fcarcely any reft.

12th and 13th. The febrile fymptoms continued, and though fhe diluted plentifully, her fkin remained parched and dry. Six grains of *James's Powder* were then adminiftered, which puked her twice, and afterwards procured her three motions : At night I directed her another powder and an emollient clyfter, with gtt. xxx. of *thebaic tincture* : She had fome fleep in the night, but no free perfpiration.

14th. In the morning apparently better, and difpofed to fleep, but towards evening, was fick at ftomach, and threw up a large quantity of bitter, glairy fluid ; in the night fhe was feized with fevere pains in her bowels, followed by feven or eight bilious ftools, and afterwards had fome fleep.

15th.

15th. Her pulfe quick, fkin dry, and her hands tremulous ; her looks were wild and ftaring, and her cheeks befet with a deep erimfon hue, fhe breathed laborioufly, and complained of great pain in her fide, and belly towards the navel : At night fhe had fix black, watery ftools ; after which an anodyne draught and a ftarch clyfter were directed : She feemed relieved, and flept for feveral hours.

16th. The pain in her belly and fide was but little abated ; fhe was extremely hot and reftlefs, and could not fweat ; I direct-ed three fpoonful of the following mixture to be given, which produced no perfpi-ration although fhe took it every two or three hours :

R̨.

Sal. Volat. Ammon. ʒ *i*
Succ. Limon. recent. exprefs. ʒ *ifs mifce*
Aq. Alex. fimp. ʒ *vi*
Tinct. Croci ʒ *iii*
Syr. ejufd. ʒ *fs fiat Miftura.*

17th.

17th. Much worfe, in all refpects; the pulfe being exceedingly quick, and almoft imperceptibly weak; cold, clammy fweats overfpread her breaft and face, which became now pale and death-like, and about twelve at noon fhe expired.

The *lochia* were difcharged in natural quantity, and fhe had milk in the breafts till within a day or two of her death.

DISSECTION.

When the body was opened, the next day in the evening; the inferior lateral portion of the *omentum* was found much inflamed, its veffels being turgid, and, as it were injected with blood, but the greater part of it was deftroyed by *fuppuration*; what remained, adhered to the fmall inteftines; which were alfo flightly cemented to each other, where their convolutions came in contact.

The

The *uterus* was contracted to the size of a large fist, and lay at the bottom of the pelvis; the *fundus uteri* seemed to partake of the general inflammation which had apparently first affected the *omentum*, and afterwards superficially overspread the *intestines, mysentery* and contiguous parts; but on cutting into its substance, it was perfectly firm and sound, although it had a livid appearance towards the cervix and os internum, which might probably be owing to the violence sustained by those parts in the time of labor.

In the cavity of the pelvis was found above a pint of *Whey-colored fluid*, with three or four ounces of *thick matter*, which did not uniformly mix with it, but floated in it like curds in whey, together with several bits of black, coagulated blood.

The *liver* was found, but remarkably pale, and the gall-bladder turgid with a large quantity of *olive-colored bile*; in consistence, equal to that of honey, and with

difficulty,

difficulty, squeezed through the cyftic duct. The ftomach contained about half a pint of black, oily liquor, refembling that which was voided by ftool.

The contents of the *thorax* were found and without any morbid appearance; except a flight adhefion of the right lobe of the lungs to the pleura.

C A S E IX.

Ann Cook, aged twenty, of a delicate habit, after eafy labor was delivered in the hofpital the 13th of *March*, 1770.

The fame evening fhe complained of ficknefs at ftomach, with pain in her bowels, and paffed a reftlefs night.

14th. Continued fick at ftomach ; took the *antimonial emetic draught*, and threw up a large quantity of bilious, ropy fluid from the ftomach ; alfo had one lax ftool; after which, a broth clyfter was injected

with

with thirty drops of *thebaic tincture.* She paffed a tolerable night, perfpired moderately, and had fome refrefhing fleep.

15th. Free from pain in the bowels, and had a good night's reft.

16th. Sick at ftomach, and vomited a quantity of poraceous fluid ; her pulfe was quick, and her thirft exceffive : She took the *antimonial powders* every four or five hours, but perfpired little, and had a reftlefs night.

17th. In the morning complained of great ficknefs, and burning heat at ftomach with violent head-ach ; and threw up near a tea-cupful of dark green liquor, which feemed to be almoft *pure bile* : She had alfo five bilious motions.

At night fuddenly feized with acute pain in her fide, and great oppreffion at her breaft; being likewife almoft fuffocated with tough phlegm, which fhe could not bring up : Her pulfe was exceeding quick and fomewhat weak, and her countenance ghaftly ; but

but as fhe breathed with vaft difficulty, I directed feven ounces of blood to be taken away, and that fhe fhould draw in the fteams of warm water into her lungs at each infpiration : She afterwards took one of the antimonial powders, which occafioned her to vomit twice, and gave her two motions. She was exceeding weak, but breathed with more freedom and eafe ; An emollient, anodyne clyfter was injected, and fhe was ordered a fpoonful or two of warm fpiced wine when faint.

18th. In the morning fhe breathed with more eafe, and was free from the load at her breaft : her pulfe beat regularly, but was extremely languid : Bladders with hot water wrapped in flannels, were applied to the foles of her feet ; fhe took light nourifhment often, and now and then a fpoonful of fpiced wine.

19th. Had refrefhing flumbers the preceding night, and gained ftrength : nothing was now given but frequent nourifhment.

O

20th.

20th. Continued better; directed the following draught to be taken twice a-day, which greatly increased her strength:

℞.

    Infus. Peruv. Cort. ℥ *iſs*
    Aq. Cin. Spt. ℨ *iii*
    Spt. Lavend. c. gtt. xxx
    Confect. Alkerm. ℨ *i fiat hauſtus.*

In about a week's time ſhe was much recovered, and went out of the hoſpital the 2d of *April* in perfect health.

C A S E   X.

Philadelphia Ford, aged twenty-eight, was delivered the 14th of *March,* 1770, and well till the third day, when ſhe complained of great pain in her head, with laſſitude and inability to turn in bed : Her countenance was florid ; had a brown dry cruſt on her tongue, and unquenchable thirſt : Her appetite left her, and there was not milk enough to give ſuck. The medicines uſually adminiſtered on ſuch occaſions

cafions had but little effect ; but all the febrile fymptoms were much relieved by the
appearance of a red cutaneous fwelling o n
the joint of her great toe : In a few days,
another fwelling of a livid color appeared
below her hip ; they were poulticed and
fomented, but did not fuppurate ; the laft
threw off a black mortified flough, and
difcharged fanious ichor. I directed her a
ftrong infufion of *bark*, with *tinct. aromat.*
and by allowing her wine and good nourifhment, fhe recovered.

Ann Deufe, of a thin, weakly habit, died
of this fever, notwithftanding various remedies were tried for her relief: She had
a natural labor, and remained well for the
firft three days ; inadvertently fhe fat up
on the fourth day, and found herfelf not
well towards evening : On the fifth,
was feized with a *fhivering fit* ; the next
day complained of pain in her belly and
fide ; and on the 29th of *March* fhe died,
being the fixth day after the attack.

She

She had milk in her breasts, and the *lochial discharge* was natural.

Bleeding in this case was not thought eligible. I have not known any instance besides this, where the disease proved fatal in so short a time, when it commenced so late after delivery, being in general, then most favorable.

The body being opened, almost exactly the same morbid appearances presented as in the preceding cases ; the *omentum* was destroyed, and a large quantity of *matter*, and *purulent serum*, collected in the *abdomen*. The *intestines* were superficially inflamed, but the *uterus* and all the other *viscera* were perfectly found.

Rebecca Day, of a healthy, robust habit, after a natural delivery, was seized with the head-ach and sickness at stomach ; two days after, a *miliary eruption* appeared on her breast and body, but without relief ; for all the febrile symptoms gradually increased,

creafed, and fhe died the 25th of *April*, being the tenth day after delivery.

The *lochial difcharge* was not defective, neither was there want of milk, till after the febrile attack.

The body was opened, but as the appearance of the *affected parts* was much the fame, and only differed in degree from thofe already mentioned; a recital of particulars would be unneceffary.

C A S E XI.

Harriot Trueman, young and of a ftrong, healthy conftitution, May the 2d, was delivered of a *monftrous child*, which prefented with the arm; fo that the cafe was preternatural in a double fenfe.

As this patient was of a plethoric habit, and fubject to cough, I directed feven ounces of blood to be taken away, before the delivery was attempted; to prevent in fome meafure, the danger of inflammation, which might arife from the violence applied in turning the child.

O 3   After

After delivery, an emollient clyfter was directed, and a faline mixture with fperm. ceti and fyr. e mecon. of which fhe was to take three fpoonful every four or five hours, as occafion required ; fhe was free from pain, and had a good night.

3d. Perfpired gently, continued free from pain and fever, her cough lefs violent, and fhe paffed her water with eafe ; the mixture was continued, and a clyfter as before, given in the evening : fhe remaind eafy during the night, and refted well.

4th. Continued perfectly eafy, and paffed a good night : the *lochial difcharge* was natural, and fhe had no pain in the region of the uterus.

5th. About three in the afternoon, was feized with difficulty of breathing, and oppreffion acrofs her breaft and ftomach ; feven ounces of blood were immediately taken away, which was exceeding fizy. The ftrokes of her pulfe were weak, quick, and

and indiftinct after bleeding, but foon became lefs frequent, and more ample and ftrong; fhe found herfelf much relieved, and could then breath with freedom; was difpofed to gentle perfpiration, and refrefhing flumbers in the night; the mixture and emollient clyfter were repeated.

The fecretion of *milk* was moderate.

6th. She continued eafy, had a natural evacuation by ftool, and flept by intervals.

7th. At four in the morning, her difficulty of breathing and cough returned; fhe was fick at ftomach, vomited up a ropy, bilious fluid, and had five *black ftools*. Her pulfe was weak, frequent and intermitting; her breafts fubfided, and the milk fuddenly difappeared.

I directed a powder, with the third part of a grain of the *tartar emetic*, and a fcruple of the *pulv. Contrayer. c.* to be repeated every four or five hours after, if the firft had no fenfible operation by fweat or vomiting, and alfo an emollient clyfter.

O 4

She

She paſſed a reſtleſs night without per-ſpiration, her belly began to ſwell, and ſhe had ſeveral involuntary bilious ſtools.

8th. Reſpiration was frequent and labo-rious, pulſe quick and weak, her ſkin dry, and ſhe complained much of pains in her ſides, and acroſs her belly near the navel, at the time of drawing her breath.

I directed a fomentation to her belly and ſides, the powders to be repeated, and a ſtarch clyſter to be injected in the evening, with gtt. xxx of the *tinct. thebaic.*

She took rice water with a ſmall quan-tity of brandy, for common drink, and a ſpoonful of ſpiced wine when faint.

The involuntary purging ſtill continued violent, and ſhe had no reſt.

9th. Complained of pains in her breaſt and belly, the difficulty of breathing in-creaſed, her pulſe was quick and almoſt imperceptibly weak ; ſhe was delirious by turns ; had cold clammy ſweats on her neck and face, and about four the next morning, ſhe expired.

DISSECTION,

DISSECTION.

When the body was opened, the greateſt part of the *omentum* was ſuppurated, and converted into *thick matter* ; the remaining portion, being much inflamed and ſlightly adhering to the folds of the *inteſtines.* The cavity of the *pelvis* and *abdomen*, contained about three pints of *putrid ſerum*, with clots of concreted pus, and ſmall pieces of coagulated blood.

The *uterus* was much contracted, and ſhrunk down to the inferior part of the pelvis : its ſubſtance was found, 'tho the os tincæ was ſomewhat livid, which appearance not being conſidered as morbid, has already been taken notice of.

Scarcely any marks of inflammation appeared on the inteſtines or meſentery ; the *liver* was apparently found, and the *gallbladder* full of *yellow bile*, which had pervaded its coats, and dyed the contiguous

parts

parts of a faffron-hue ; but this I did not look upon as a morbid appearance.

The *ftomach* contained a pint of *blackifh fluid,* like that voided by ftool, and which had the appearance of putrid bile.

On raifing the fternum, two ounces or more of *matter* was lodged upon the *mediaftinum* ; and the *thorax* contained a fmall quantity of the fame kind of whey-colored fluid as that found in the abdomen : The *lungs* were apparently found, only the left lobe' adhered flightly to the pleura, at its pofterior part.

REMARKS.

The extravafion of purulent fluid in the abdomen, by hindering the free play of the diaphragm, will, in a great meafure, account for the difficulty of breathing ; particularly as the lungs were ftill further oppreffed by the fame kind of fluid in the thorax.

As

As the blackifh fluid found in the fto-mach refembled putrid bile ; I mixed a fmall quantity of it with vinegar, but could not perceive any effervefcence, neither did the vinegar change it green ; but this per-haps might be owing to the natural pro-perties of the bile being altered by putre-faction.

Hippocrates, in his Aphorifms, takes no-tice, that *black excrements*, refembling black blood, are to be looked upon as a bad omen ; and that *black bile* rejected either upwards or downwards at the beginning of a difeafe, is a *mortal fign* ; which obferva-tion is verified by repeated experience in the advanced ftate of difeafes, as well as at their beginning.*

The color of the excrements paffing through the alimentary tube, principally depends upon the quantity and quality of *bile* ; thus, where there is a defect of it, the ftools are pale, and the body coftive, and

* *Hippocrat.* Aphorifm. Sect. quart. Aphor. 21 et 22.

and on the contrary, when it abounds, they
are yellow or greenifh, and generally fre-
queut.

Black, fœtid ftcols, fuch as were obferved towards the end of *Child-bed Fever*,
almoft certainly denote *internal mortification*, and therefore, it is no wonder they
were fo often followed by a fatal conclufion ; but fuch a mortification cannot affect the color of the excrements, except by means of the bile, which after
abforption of the corrupted fluids into the
blood, will at laft become putrid, black,
and acrimonious.

There was fomething very fingular in
this woman's child, which was *monftrous* :
It had no thumbs ; the parietal bones were
wanting ; and not above two ounces of
brain was found in the cavity of the fcull :
The upper part of the fcalp adhered ftrongly to the internal furface of the *placenta*,
fo that when the child was extracted, this
part was pulled along with it, though
luckily

luckily, it was not attended with any degree of flooding.

Elizabeth Pool, young, and of a healthy conftitution, was delivered the 15th of *May,* and foon after affected with the fymptoms of this fever, but in a degree lefs acute than ufual : Her cafe was much like that of *Elizabeth Waters* ; for though fhe laboured under a flow, lingering fever for a long time, her appetite remained.

She was deprived of the ufe of her limbs for feveral days, yet the fevere pains of which fhe complained, were not, like thofe of the former, followed by abfceffes in the mufcular parts.

On the 16th of *June* fhe was fufficiently recovered to go out of the Hofpital.

About this time, as near as I can recollect, I was called to a gentlewoman at *Clapham,* who was feized with this fever ; and notwithftanding fhe had been very properly treated by her apothecary, and took every

thing

thing that could be devifed for her fafety, fhe died about the tenth day after the attack.

C A S E   XII.

Mrs. *P—*, a lady in *Holborn*, aged twenty-eight, and of a delicate habit of body, was delivered by her midwife on *Saturday* morning the 7th of July, 1770.

The birth was not attended with any dangerous or uncommon circumftance; fhe was eafy after delivery, and refted well at night.

8th. Towards evening, complained of head-ach, but had feveral hours fleep the following night.

9th. Waked in the morning with *acute pain* in her right fide, her head-ach was worfe, and about three in the afternoon, fhe had a violent *fhivering fit*, with coldnefs of the extremities, and great internal heat acrofs her breaft and ftomach : I found her pulfe exceeding quick, her head-ach violent, her tongue white and dry, and the

pain

pain in her fide extremely acute and deep feated ; fhe breathed laborioufly, and had no perfpiration, except on the breaft and face.

I directed eight ounces of blood to be taken away, and one of the *antimonial powders* to be given, which was to be repeated every two or three hours, if the firft had no effect. An emollient clyfter was adminiftered, and bladders of warm water were applied to the foles of her feet and fides ; She paffed a reftlefs night, without any abatement of pain or difficulty of breathing.

Two of the powders were taken, the firft created naufea, but did not prove emetic, nor produce any confiderable perfpiration.

The blood was not fo fizy as I expected.

10th. The pulfe being full, hard, and frequent, her fkin dry, and refpiration difficult and painful ; eight ounces more blood were drawn ; the powders were repeated every

every four or five hours, and a *blister* was applied to the affected fide in the evening: She drank plentifully of common emulfion with *nitre*, to prevent ftrangury, and relieve her difficulty of making water, which had been troublefome from the beginning

11th. Had no fleep the preceding night; and as the pain in her head and difficulty of breathing ftill increafed, fhe was again blooded in the night, to the quantity of fix ounces, as I had previoufly directed, in cafe the fymptoms became urgent.

She was much relieved foon after this laft bleeding; the pain abated; fhe could then breathe with more freedom, her pulfe became more foft and lefs frequent, and a free and equal perfpiration broke out all over her body.

At this time fhe began to be troubled with a cough, and was much opprefled with white, vifcid phlegm, which was expectorated with great difficulty; fhe had

two

two motions with a large difcharge of fœces, which came away with the fecond clyfter.

. The laft drawn blood was uncommonly fizy, and the *gelatinous cruft* on its furface extremely thick and tenacious.

She had milk in her breafts, which were drawn twice a-day, and the *lochial difcharge* was natural.

As fhe perfpired freely, the powders were difcontinued, and the *faline draughts*, with *oxymel fcillit.* given every five or fix hours.

The blifter rofe well ; the emulfion was continued, and the emollient clyfter ordered to be repeated as before.

About nine at night all her feverifh fymptoms returned ; her pulfe was exceeding quick, fkin dry, her thirft intolerable, and the pain in her fide, and difficulty of breathing were fo violent, that her *apothecary* was called up in the night, and took away fix ounces more blood : One of the

P

antimonial

antimonial powders was also given, after which she again began to perspire, with an abatement of all the feverish symptoms, and had two or three hours refreshing sleep.

12th. Something better ; but in the evening was attacked with a deep-seated violent pain in her other side, between the breast and axilla, so as almost to prevent her from breathing ; her cough was troublesome, and she expectorated with much difficulty ; four ounces more blood were drawn, and the following draught prescribed :

℞

    Sal. Volat. ammon. gr. xv

    Succ. Limon. ʒ *iii*

    Aq. alex. simp. ℥ *i*

    ---*Spt. cum Acet.* ʒ *ii*

    *Tinct. Thebaic. g*ᵗᵗ*. xii*

    Syr. e. Mecon. ʒ *i*

Misce & fiat haustus vesperi exhibendus.

She drank plentifully of thin diluting liqors with *nitre* ; the clyster was repeated

as

as before, and by intervals, she took the following mixture :

℞

 Sperm. Ceti solut. ℥ *ii*
 Lact. ammon. ℥ *vii*
 Elix. Paregoric. ℥ *iii fiat mistura.*

Had an exceeding bad night, but slumbered a little at times.

13th. Apparently better, but complained of severe rheumatic pains about her back and loins : Her cough was more and more troublesome, and greatly interrupted her rest, but was relieved by the mixture with *gum ammoniacum*, to which a small quantity of *oxymel Scillit.* was added.

White wine whey was ordered to be given her in the night to support her strength, and she took a decoct. of bread with currant jelly for nourishment.

14th. Had two or three hours refreshing sleep the preceding night, and the feverish symptoms were somewhat abated ; but an there was not yet the least sediment or se-

paration

paration in her urine, which was high-colored, I still referred the use of *bark*, and directed the anodyne draught at night as before, which always eased her cough, and procured sleep.

15th. Being *Sunday*, about two in the morning, her relations thought her in great danger, and particularly requested me to see her, which I did accordingly : Her pulse was quick and tremulous, her extremities cold, and her face and breasts were be-dewed with a clammy sweat. She breathed laboriously, with convulsive jerks, and complained of great weight and op-pression across her breast : though per-fectly sensible, she had a wild, eager countenance, a trembling hand, and appa-rently all the symptoms of approaching death.

I gave her four spoonfuls of a strong cor-dial julep, ordered sinapisms to her feet ; her extremities were rubbed with hot flan-nels; and cloths dipped in brandy were applied to her stomach.   A

A few hours after I was gone, she revived, but grew restless and almost frantic, insisting upon cold water to drink, which was given her: The next day I was acquainted she was still alive; when I visited her about one in the afternoon, she was perfectly sensible, but so weak and languid that she was scarcely able to speak.

I directed a cordial julep to be given when faint, and the following draught with *bark*, to be taken every two hours, or as often as her stomach would bear; but as she had several involuntary motions, I ordered five grains of the *pil. e styrace* to be instantly given, which restrained the looseness, and procured some hours sleep, before the bark could be prepared.

℞

> *Decoct. Peruv. Cort.* ℥ *iss*
> *Pulv. subtiliss. ejusd.* ℨ *ss*
> *Aq. Cinn. Spt.* ℨ *iii*
> *Syr. e Mecon.* ℨ *i*
> *fiat haustus alternis horis exhibendus.*

By

By eleven o'clock at night, fhe had taken four draughts, and had very little return of fever ; but as her fkin was dry and thirft intenfe, I allowed her to drink plentifully of toaft and water, which fhe particularly defired, and fwallowed with great eagernefs ; after which, fhe gently perfpired towards the morning, and growing cooler began the draughts as before. The urine was amber colored, but without fediment or feparation.

16th. Better in all refpects, but very weak, and her reft much difturbed in the night by the cough : Draughts continued as before, and by intervals wine and light nourifhment were given often, and in fmall quantities.

17th. Continued free from fever, and able to fit up ; fhe had three ftools, was much difturbed by her cough, and complained of a fore throat.

Directed

Directed *pil. e ſtyrace* three grains, and the draughts only to be given three times a-day.

There was no remarkable change 'till the 21ſt. at which time ſhe was almoſt unable to ſwallow, her throat being much worſe, and the tonſil glands ſlightly ulcerated; her cough was troubleſome, and ſeveral *miliary eruptions* appeared in her body.

The following draught was given every four or five hours, and her throat was fumigated with the ſteams of hot vinegar poured on lavender flowers, which gave her great relief.

℞

      Decoct. Cort. Peruv. ℥ iſs

      Extract. ejuſd. moll. Ð i

      Elix. Vitriol. dulc. g^{tt} xx.

      Aq. Cin. Spt. ℥ iii

Confect. Alkerm. ℥ i. *miſce & fiat hauſtus.*

Her ſtrength was ſupported by nouriſhment of eaſy digeſtion as often as her ſtomach

mach

mach would difpenfe with it, and a little fpiced claret was given whenever fhe pleafed.

23d. I defired fhe might be removed into the country (*Clapham*) for the benefit of air; and in a few days fhe was fo much better in all refpects, as to leave off her medicines, and only took a tincture of *bark*, and *cardamons* as a ftomachic, in a ftrong infufion of *tanfy*.

REMARKS.

This fever was complicated with the *pleurify* in a high degree; a cafe, of all others the moft dangerous; and as pleuritic fymptoms do fometimes accompany a morbid affection of the *abdominal vifcera* in this difeafe; perhaps it might reafonably be afked, whether the *diarrhæa* and *inflammation of the omentum*, which fo ufually fucceeded the *rigor*, were not here prevented by *early* and *repeated bleeding ?*

From

From what may be obferved in the fore-going hiftory; *it does not appear eligible to wait for a diftinct intermiffion of this fever, left a fevere attack of the febrile paroxyfm fhould in the mean time carry off the patient* : I think a remiffion of the fymptoms, efpecially if attended with any critical evacuation, is, in general, fufficient to juftify the liberal and immediate ufe of the *bark* ; but where they are at firft manifeftly inflammatory, when bleeding and evacuations had not preceded ; I have feen it given without any good effect.

C A S E.   XIII.

Sarah Evans, about twenty-one years of age, was delivered in the Hofpital on *Monday* the 19th of *November*, 1770 ; fhe had a natural labor, and was well the two firft days after delivery ; but on the third day feized with fever, which the *matron* believed was owing to a furprize, as the febrile fymptoms appeared very foon after.

As

As this patient was of a very delicate irritable habit, and lax fibres, I did not think it proper to direct bleeding, particularly as her skin was moist, and her pulse quick and weak.

She took a mixture with *spt. mindereri* and the *tinct. thebaic* ; emollient clysters were also directed to be frequently administered. After the fever had gradually increased for a few days, she complained of difficulty of breathing, and pain in the side of her belly, towards the navel. Warm flannels were applied to the part affected, and bladders of hot water to her feet.

She drank beef water, and weak pimento tea for common drink ; and being extremely languid, was allowed a small quantity of white wine and light nourishment by turns.

On the 29th of *November* she was still weaker ; the heart almost ceasing to do its office, and the circulation being at the lowest ebb. The next morning she calmly expired

expired without any figns of mortal an-
guifh.

DISSECTION.

On opening the body, evident marks
of inflammation appeared, particularly in
the *abdomen* : Great part of the *omentum*
was deftroyed, and converted into *matter*,
what remained was become *gangrenous* ; its
difeafed membranous expanfions here and
there overfpread the *inteftines*, and flightly
adhered to their furface, which was alfo
inflamed, particularly at their convolutions ; thofe parts, from the additional
effect of preffure, being as it were fuperfi-
cially foldered together : That portion of
the *omentum* which is inferted round the
great curvature of the ftomach, was alfo
confiderably inflamed.

The *uterus* had a natural appearance, and
was perfectly found, as well as all the parts
peculiar to it.

The

The *liver* was also unaffected, except its peritonæal coat, which being diffolved by the inflammation, lay on its furface in a tender, gelatinous ftate. The *gall-bladder* was turgid with *bile.*

The *mediaftinum* was inflamed, but the *lungs* were perfectly found, and free from adhefion to the pleura.

The *whey-colored, putrid fluid* contained in the cavity of the abdomen, was nearly the fame in quantity and appearance as that in the former cafes.

Where the pulfe was extremely foft and weak, and the circulation languid; it is difficult to account for fo fudden and high a degree of inflammation, as to produce a collection of *matter,* or any inflammatory affection of the abdominal vifcera; but fo it was; and therefore, in all fuch cafes, where bleeding feems improper, it will be requifite, immediately to apply *finapifms,* or a *large blifter* to the *umbilical region.*

CASE.

CASE XIV.

Hannah Jeffreys, of a ftrong, healthy conftitution ; the fourth day after delivery,
which was natural, was feized with a *fhivering fit*, fucceeded by head-ach, and great
ficknefs at ftomach, with fix bilious ftools;
fhe was affected with univerfal languor, and
dejection of fpirits, was very reftlefs, and
had a fmart, quick pulfe.

A clyfter with beef-water was given, and
fhe diluted plentifully with warm balm-tea,
but did not perfpire.

The next morning, fhe had two purgative evacuations, and labored under much
anxiety and oppreffion at her breaft : Broad,
purple colored fpots which rofe a little above
the furface of her fkin, foon after appeared
all over her body, they were very thick on
her breaft and face, but not attended with
any mitigation of the fymptoms, except
for an hour or two in the beginning.

She took one of the *antimonial powders*,
which was repeated every three or four
hours

hours, without any sensible evacuation whatever : As she was no better in the evening, the eruption appearing *livid*, and her extremities being cold ; a cordial julep was given her now and then ; *blisters* were applied to the inside of her arms, and *cataplasms* to her feet ; the emollient clyster was repeated, and she was allowed white-wine whey for common drink.

The two following days all the febrile symptoms increased, with the difficulty of breathing ; altho' the blisters, which had been applied, produced their proper effect ; and thus growing gradually worse and worse, she died at four in the morning, on the 5th of *May*, 1771, being the ninth day from that of her delivery.

R E M A R K S.

The causes from whence those *petechiæ* are said to happen, are so different, as to make a difference in their treatment, very essential to the patient's safety ; for instance, inftance, if they arife from putrid diffolution of the blood, they will require the ufe of *bark*, with *acids* ; and all fuch medicines as confirm its texture, and refift the putre-factive tendency prevailing in the habit ; but if, on the contrary, they are produced by too violent a degree of the circulating power, which may occafion rupture of the fmall arteries, and extravafation of the fan-guineous globules, then the former remedies are to be avoided ; and fuch as diminifh the action of the heart and arteries, will afford the moft relief ; viz. *bleeding*, *fedatives*, and cooling regimen.

The firft cafe is attended with exceeding danger, and very often proves fatal: Here the pulfe is generally quick and weak, and the lofs of ftrength great and fudden ; on the contrary, in the fecond cafe, the pulfe is hard and full, the artery vibrates more ftrongly, and the *fpots* may fometimes be found, by the touch, to rife a little above

the

the furface of the fkin, which is ufually hot and florid ; but it muft be confeffed, that fome particular fevers are fo indiftinctly marked, as to their fpecies, and their fymptoms fo complicated and equivocal, that it is not a little difficult to know with certainty from what caufes they arife.

This laft cafe was the only one where the *omentum* was neither fuppurated, or become gangrenous ; there was indeed, fome figns of flight inflammation, and a confiderable quantity of fluid in the *abdomen*, which looked like the *ferum* of blood ; but it was not purulent, as in the former cafes. Hence it is probable, that a gradual accumulation of fluid in the *abdomen* commences before death, as the *lymphatics* lofe their abforbent power, from defect of the *vis vitæ*.

We have been told, the body has fometimes been obferved to remain warm for feveral days after death, and that the limbs, inftead of becoming ftiff and rigid, continue

tinue foft and flexible : This extraordinary circumftance occurred to me once or twice, and occafioned no fmall anxiety in the friends of the deceafed, who looked upon it as a fign of fome latent fparks of life, and therefore would not permit interment of the body, until long after the ufual time. But in reality, fuch appearances are ftrictly *morbid*, and inftead of creating hope, fhould totally exclude it ; for they denote difeafes highly putrid, and of a mortal nature. All animal bodies tend to diffolution, as foon as the progreffive motion of their fluids ceafes ; and this preternatural heat of body feems owing to nothing but an uncommon degree of *putrefactive fermentation* which is known to generate *heat*.

The following cafe was drawn up by Mr. *Patten*, furgeon to the fhip Refolution which failed round the world, commanded by the late *Captain Cook*.

Q

CASE

CASE XV.

Sibyl Watson, aged twenty-two, was delivered in the Hofpital Oct. 2d, 1776, of her firft child, without any uncommon circumftance attending the labor which was eafy and natural : The placenta came away without any affiftance, about ten minutes after delivery. She refted well in the night, and perfpired gently.

This woman was of a lax and delicate conftitution, and had during the two laft months of pregnancy, been troubled with a flight pain in her left fide attended with cough and difficulty of breathing, but thefe complaints had in a great meafure been removed by bleeding fome time before delivery.

3d. In the morning fhe was perfectly free from pain and fever, but about fix in the evening without any apparent caufe, was fuddenly attacked with burning heat diffufed all over her body, which was fucceeded by coldnefs and fhivering, great

anxiety

anxiety and oppreſſion at the *præcordia*, and univerſal pain. For theſe complaints ſhe took a few drops of the tinctura thebaica in a little mint water.

At nine, when I ſaw her, ſhe had the following ſymptoms, *viz.* violent pain in the left ſide of the thorax, which ſtruck down to the left groin, ſometimes to the right, and frequently darted from thence to the navel. She had great ſoreneſs all over the abdomen, a frequent nauſea and retching to vomit, which brought up nothing but phlegm; her breathing was ſhort, and laborious, the pulſe quick, weak, and unequal, ſometimes fluttering, and at other times regular, with ſome ſmall degree of hardneſs; her voice was weak and tremulous, her countenance pale, the ſkin hard and rough, without the leaſt moiſture on any part of her body, except the breaſt and neck; ſhe complained at intervals of acute pain in the ſtomach,

Q 2

which

which continued for a fhort time, but frequently returned ; fhe had alfo a fixed pain
in the right fhoulder.

Dr. *Leake* directed ten ounces of blood to
be taken from the arm, which gave her
immediate relief ; the pulfe became more
regular, and the oppreffion about the præcordia, and difficulty of breathing, were almoft totally removed. The fourth part
of a grain of emetic tartar was given with
the faline draught every three or four
hours, and fhe drank plentifully of warm
diluting liquors.

4th. No reft the preceding night ;
in the morning fhe had a bilious ftool, her
pulfe was full and quick, attended with
difficult refpiration, and great oppreffion at
the præcordia, with frequent fighings ; her
tongue was white, but moift, and fhe complained of univerfal pain and forenefs all
over the abdomen : The tartar emetic was
continued, with large dofes of camphorated julep every three hours ; fhe diluted plentifully, but did not perfpire.

5th

5th.   Had eight bilious ftools, the pain and difficulty of breathing were confiderably abated, her complexion more lively, the pulfe regular, differing little from a healthy ftate, a gentle moifture was diffufed over the whole body ; fhe had a moderate fecretion of milk, and the lochia were difcharged in their natural quantity. Two ounces of a ftrong decoction of bark were now prefcribed and directed to be given every four hours ; fhe refted well in the night, and perfpired gently.

6th. Had five bilious ftools without pain, and was much better in all refpects. The decoction of bark was continued.

7th. Almoft every complaint vanifhed ; fhe was fo much better, as to be able to walk about the ward without affiftance, and in due time was difcharged from the Hofpital perfectly recovered.

Q 3   CASE

C A S E XVI.

Sarah Davies was delivered at the Weſt-minſter Lying-In Hoſpital, December 4th, 1778. The lochial diſcharge and excretions in general were natural.

8th. The pulſe full and frequent ; reſpiration difficult.   She was thirſty, had pain in her head, and as ſhe expreſſed it, at her heart alſo.   By the matron's order, balm tea and barley water were given for common drink.

9th. She was viſited by *Dr. Leake*, who preſcribed the antimonial powders and bottles of warm water to her feet.

11th. Better in every reſpect, with abatement of thirſt, perſpiration moderate, the bowels laxative, and pulſe not ſo quick.

12th. Worſe, as ſuppoſed, from anxiety of mind ; pulſe low and frequent, the jaws ſtrongly contracted, and breathing difficult, with pain in her bowels and looſe offenſive ſtools.   *Dr. Leake* directed a bliſter to the ſide, fide, and bolus's of *camphor, mufk and opium,* which were given when they could be got into her mouth.

13th. Pulfe low and quick, and ftools frequent, fame medicines continued.

14th. Purging more violent, attended with flow fever, thirft violent and fkin dry. Vifited by *Dr. Leake,* who directed a cold infufion of bark and antimonial powders.

15th and 16th. Delirious in the night, ftools fœtid, pulfe quick and languid. Antimonials omitted, and the camphorated julep ordered to be given often, with a ftrong infufion of cortex.

17th. Much the fame. Medicines continued.

18th. Worfe in the night, the abdomen much fwelled, ftools black, fœtid and involuntary. The medicines were continued as long as fhe could take them, and an opiate at night was given.

19th. In the morning the patient died.

Dr.

Dr. Leake directed the body to be opened, the next day at night, in the prefence of *fixteen gentlemen* of the faculty. The abdominal integuments being removed, the omentum was found inflamed on one fide. The inteftines were much diftended with wind, efpecially the colon. On the ftomach was found a fmall, gangrenous fpot. The other vifcera, as well as thofe of the thorax, had no difeafed appearance.

The contents of the pelvis were found, and the uterus contracted to the fize of a fmall melon. After this examination the *Section of the Symphyfis Pubis* was performed, in order to afcertain *how much fpace might be gained between the divided bones.*

The cartilage being laid bare, by Mr. *Poignand,* furgeon, an obfcure motion was perceived between the bones upon moving the thigh up and down, and the cartilage being very foft, was then cut through by *Dr. Leake,* with great eafe and without wounding the neck of the bladder,

bladder, or any of the contiguous parts. The ossa-pubis immediately receded from each other about one inch, and with very gentle force were feperated *two inches and an eighth*. The contents of the pelvis were afterwards removed, and on examining the *internal, posterior ligaments* of the bones of the pelvis, they were neither lacerated or in the least injured.

This operation gave general satisfaction to the gentlemen prefent, of whom, as a pupil, and *Hofpital Affiftant to Dr. Leake*, I had the honor to be one.

From the circumstances attending this cafe, where no part effential to life was cut or injured, Dr. *Leake* as well as the reft of the gentlemen, were inclined to think the fection of the pubes, in fafety and advantage, preferable to the Cæfarian operation,

J. Lawton.

Weftminfter New-Lying-Inn Hofpital,
  December 15th, 1778.

Several

Several other medical gentlemen and pupils intended to have been prefent at this operation, but were prevented by receiving intelligence too late.

With refpect to the number of patients delivered, and likewife thofe who died in the *Weftminfter New lying-in-hofpital*; the account, as appears by the Hofpital books, ftands thus: From the 20th of *April*, 1767, to the 30th of *November*, 1769; out of *two hundred and eighty-five* delivered, three had the *Child-bed Fever*, of whom, *Eliz. Waters*, and *Eliz. Becket* recovered, and *Sufannah Vernon*, who had twins, died; alfo *Ann Moody*, of the *fmall pox* the day after delivery.

From the foregoing date, to the 15th of *May*, 1770, (being the *epidemic feafon*) out of fixty-three delivered, *nineteen* had the *Child-bed Fever*, befides others more flightly affected with it; of which number, eleven died in the hofpital, and two more out of the houfe, who were removed at the requeft of

their

their friends ; namely, *Frances Williams* and *Mary Gammon.* *Elizabeth Kibblewhite,* alfo died of inflammation in her bowels, during the above period.

From the 15th of *May,* 1770, to the 29th of *September,* 1772, out of *three hundred and five* delivered, two died, viz. *Sarah Evans,* and *Hannah Jeffreys.*

This fever was alfo *epidemical* in *London* in the year 1760, of which, twenty four died in the *Britifh Lying-Inn-Hofpital,* from the 12th of *June,* to the latter end of *December* ; there being no inftance of any fuch mortality in fo fhort a time, till the year 1770, when it was again extremely fatal.

THE SECTION OF THE PUBES firft propofed by *M. Sigault* in his *Thefis* at *Angiers,* and afterwards by him fuccefsfully performed on the living body at Paris, Sept. 2d. 1777, having lately much engaged the attention of Medical Gentlemen, I fhall beg leave to offer fome general Animadverfions on that new and extraordinary operation ;

particularly

particularly as *M. Le Roy*, Profeffor of Midwifery, and doctor regent of the faculty of phyfic at Paris, who affifted him in the performance of it, was pleafed to honor me with his *Treatife on that fubject* ; and as *Mr. Poignand* the Tranflator has thought fit to addrefs it to me.

Mr. *Sigault* fuppofes that the cartilages interpofed between the bones of the pelvis become relaxed by the effect of pregnancy, and therefore that they recede from each other in the time of labor, by the preffure of the *child's head*. He defcribes the Section of the Pubes and propofes it as a fubftitute for the *Cæfarian operation* ; the propriety of which, as well as the objections brought againft it, I am defirous to examine with attention and candor ; for little advantage can arife from opinions, where men rather contend for fuperiority than truth. The fpirit of enquiry is only commendable when it is exerted for the improvement of fcience, and folely directed

for

for the *public good*. But although, I am inclined to think favorably of this operation, for reafons hereafter affigned, I know that nothing but time and future experience can fufficiently determine whether it ought to be rejected or adopted.

The ftructure of the parts on which this operation is performed, being perfectly known to every medical reader, their defcription, as well as that of the operation itfelf, would be unneceffary, efpecially as the laft is circumftantially fet down in Mr. Le Roy's tract, entitled *Practical Enquiries on the Section of the Pubes*, to which I muft refer him.

The following are the objections to this *New Operation*; Firft, that the cartilage at the fymphyfis of the pubes, may happen to be *offified*, which would prevent its divifion by the knife : Secondly, that the neck of the bladder may be wounded : Thirdly ; that the fpace gained by the fection of the Pubes, may not, in a narrow pelvis, be fufficient

cient to allow the child's head to descend through the cavity : Fourthly; that the union of the cartilage may not be affected : And lastly, that the *internal, posterior ligaments uniting the sacrum and ilia,* may be torn asunder, by dividing the bones of the pubes.

In answer to the preceding objections : First, it may be remarked that cartilage being a substance essentially distinct from bone, is never found ossified except in a *præternatural state,* or in *old age,* after the time of child-bearing is past, and where there could be no occasion for the operation. I cannot however, assent to the opinion of *Sigault,* that the cartilages of the pelvis, undergo a temporary change, and become softer in the time of pregnancy. The obscure motion perceived at the symphysis of the pubes, in the patient at the *Westminster Lying-in Hospital,* already mentioned, I believe was not owing to any additional softness, but entirely to its own permanent structure as a cartilage

cartilage which allowed of obscure motion, when considerable force was applied.

Secondly, the neck of the bladder being only slightly attached to the symphysis of the pubes, by cellular membrane, and not in close union with the cartilage; there *never can be the least danger of wounding it*, except the operator is unskilful and ignorant of the structure and situation of the parts.

Thirdly, the space only of *one inch* gained by *M. Sigault* from the section of the pubes, on the dead body, does not appear sufficient to enlarge the bony passage for the exit of a child's head, in a pelvis uncommonly narrow; but in the case of Mrs. Brasier, *M. Le Roy* found a separation of *two inches and a half*; and as the case at the *Westminster Lying-in Hospital* affords incontestible proof, that after the section of the cartilage, the bones of the pubes, without violence receded from each other, full *two inches and an eighth*, I have no doubt but

so

ſo much additional ſpace, would in general be ſufficient to let the child's head paſs, even in a pelvis ſo preternaturally narrow, that no other means but the *Cæſarian operation* could be deviſed for its birth.

Of all the cauſes of difficult labor, the moſt frequent and invincible obſtacle to child-birth is that of a *narrow or diſtorted pelvis*; to remedy which, the *Section of the Pubes* ſeems more peculiarly adapted; but here we are told by ſome that although the *long axis* of the pelvis may from thence be extended from ſide to ſide, its *ſhorteſt diameter* from *ſacrum to Pubes,* where additional ſpace is moſt wanted, will not be increaſed in the ſame proportion, and therefore the operation cannot avail. This indeed, at firſt ſight, looks like a ſpecious and inſurmountable ob_jection, which if not duly attended to, and thoroughly examined, might greatly depreciate the merit and advantages of the new operation. I ſhall, therefore, beg the Reader's attention to the following circumſtances, which

which if clearly underſtood, I preſume will diſprove and totally ſet aſide what has ſo plauſibly been alledged againſt it. By the *Section of the Pubes*, it is now generally allowed, even by its opponents, that the ſpace gained by the aperture between the divided bones, is nearly *two inches and a half*, even in the dead body, where the parts are cold, and rigid, and conſequently leſs yielding than in a living ſtate. It will therefore follow, that as much of the occiput or hind head as is protruded into an aperture at the pubes of *two inches and a half; ſo much preciſely will be the ſpace gained by this operation, and ſuperadded to the ſhort axis of the pelvis, from ſacrum to pubes* ; and ſince the occiput preſenting at the ſymphyſis is much ſmaller in diameter than the head itſelf ; ſo much greater will be its projection into the aperture ; and therefore the ſpace gained from ſacrum to pubes will be equal to the enlargement of the pelvis from ſide to ſide; which is the circumſtance here contended

R   for

for, and what we presume is fully proved, contrary to the assertion of those, who have opposed the new operation.

Fourthly, from the observations, and un-questionable authority of *Petit* and *De La Faye*, we are assured, that *cartilages will as firmly unite after division*, as bones after a fracture. But, to put this matter out of all doubt, *Camper*, a Dutch physician, made experiment upon a quadruped, by cutting through the cartilage of the *pubes*, and after dissecting the parts, he found they were *firmly united*.

Lastly, respecting the pretended laceration of the internal, posterior ligaments of the pelvis uniting the sacrum to the ilia, I must refer to the case at the *Westminster-Hospital*, already recited, where the section of the pubes was made in the presence of *sixteen Medical Gentlemen*, and where, notwithstanding the space gained was *two inches and an eighth*; no laceration or the least marks of violence appeared, but on the

contrary,

contrary, thofe ligaments were found perfectly firm, and in their natural ftate. If
fo much fpace could be obtained without
laceration in the *dead body*, where the fibres
were cold and rigid, and their cohefion confiderably weakened by natural tendency to
diffolution ; how much greater fpace might
reafonably have been expected in the living
fubject, where the folids are more foft and
yielding ?

That thefe ligaments may be torn afun-
der by forcibly pulling open the bones
of the pubes, cannot be denied ; but
the fame thing will happen to a fhip's
cable, whenever a force more than equal
to its refiftance is applied. In fhort, with
any reafonable degree of prudent caution,
the laceration of thefe ligaments need never be apprehended.

Let us now take a comparative view of the
Cæfarian operation, for the fuccefs of which,
Rouffetus contends with fo much zeal; whilft
Marchant condemns the operation as highly

R 2   dangerous,

gerous, and informs us that *Pare*, *Guillemeau*, *Viard*, and others of the first rank in their profession, found this operation extremely unsuccessful.

In the fourth volume of the London Medical Observations, may be found a case of *Cæsarian operation* accurately related, and the only instance that I know of, where it was performed upon the *living body*, in this great city, for upwards of a century past. From this case, as one which may be depended upon, I have transcribed the following particulars, being the leading circumstances, and most material, practical facts relative to the nature and event of that operation.

The *Cæsarian operation* was performed on *Martha Rhodes*, Oct. 21st. 1769, by Mr. Thomson, surgeon to the London Hospital, who informs us, that the patient did not lose more than four ounces of blood, though she died about five hours after. The body being opened, grumous blood which was computed to weigh about twenty ty ounces, was found on the furface of the *omentum* and *uterus.* The cavity of the womb alfo contained blood, fo that the whole quantity of this vital fluid loft by the operation was allowed to be *thirty ounces.* Mr. Thomfon fays, it is well known, that in natural labors, the difcharge of blood will often much exceed that quantity ; and therefore feems at a lofs to form a judgment what might have been the immediate caufe of this patient's fudden death.

From this laft opinion I muft beg leave very much to differ ; but even admitting the quantity of blood difcharged in a natural labor to be confiderable, as it fometimes is ; the danger fhould not be eftimated fimply by its quantity, but by the *fhort fpace of time in which it is difcharged, as well as the nature of the blood itfelf, and the fource from which it is derived.*

After delivery, the blood is very flowly evacuated from the innumerable fmall veffels proceeding from the womb, and enter-

R 3   ing

ing the cellular fubſtance of the placenta, for the immediate *ſervice of the child*; reſpecting the mother, this blood may therefore be looked upon as *redundant, and not eſſential to the ſupport of her own body.* On the contrary, in the *Cæſarian ſection*, where the large dilated arteries and veins of the womb are divided, and *thirty ounces* of vital blood, or that merely, *maternal*, ſuddenly guſhes forth in a full ſtream, I am inclined to think that ſo powerful a check to the circulation, may ſuſpend the heart's motion, and prove the immediate cauſe of the patient's death, by producing a mortal ſyncope; particularly, when we conſider, that the *hypogaſtric arteries* entering the uterus, proceed from large branches of the *aorta*, through which the blood circulates with extreme velocity.

But could we ſuppoſe the patient might eſcape a *mortal hæmorrhage*, after this operation; would not the large quantity of grumous blood evtravaſated in the cavity of

the

the belly, from which it could not be evacuated, corrupt and deftroy the contiguous vital parts, and prove the *remote caufe of her death* ?

The *Section of the Pubes*, which allows the child to be born by the natural paffage, carries not with it thofe ideas of cruelty which attend the *Cæfarian Operation*, where the patient is, as it were, emboweled alive. No formidable apparatus is neceffary ; the fection being made with expedition, and without pain or danger ; no blood-veffel, nerve, or other parts effential to life are wounded ; thefe divided, being only *cutis, cellular membrane and infenfible cartilage,* from which neither *Hæmorrhage,* or *fymptomatic Fever,* are to be apprehended.

Thefe are my reafons for preferring the *New Operation,* by which the mother and child may probably *both be faved* ; but where the mother at leaft, to whofe fafety our principal attention fhould be directed, would generally be loft by the Cæfarian Section.   R 4

To

To those who vaguely give it as their opinion that this operation will not succeed, the answer is short ; *it has already succeeded, and therefore it will again succeed* ; particularly with such as are disposed to give it *fair and judicious trial* ; but it will be prudent for every *Accoucheur*, not rashly to undertake this, or any other capital operation, on the living body, without the concurrence, and assistance of others of the profession eminent for their candor and skill.

M. Le Roy gives several examples of its success. *M. Despree*, surgeon, in *Britanny*, performed the section of the pubes with happy event in 1778 ; and *Monf. De Lambon*, first surgeon to the Duchess of Lorraine, in a letter to *Monf. De Brambilla*, lately published at *Mons*, informs him that he had performed the section of the pubes on two patients, *with success* ; one of which submitted to the operation *twice*, and is now in perfect health, as well as her child, of which she was happily delivered by the *second operation*.

My

My ingenious friend, Dr. *Haufman*, of *Brunfwick*, who did me the honor to number himfelf among my pupils, obliged me with a manufcript account of this operation fuccefsfully performed by Profeffor *Siebold:* His recital of this cafe, refpecting its favourable event, is very different from what it appears in a periodical publication, but whether this may be owing to miftake or other caufes, I cannot take upon me to fay, as I have not yet had an opportunity of feeing the original cafe related by *M. Siebold.*

To conclude refpecting the cafe of Mrs. *Souchot*, upon whom the fection of the pubes was firft performed by *M. Sigault*, fuch was the event, that both the mother and child were preferved; the circumftances appeared fo extraordinary, that Commiffioners were appointed by the *Medical Faculty of Paris*, to examine into the ftate of the cafe and fuccefs attending it, in confequence of which, the honor of prize medals was conferred on *M. Sigault*, as well as *M. Le Roy*, who affifted him in the operation.   S E C-

SECTION V.

Of the Nature and Treatment of Uterine Hæmorrhages, before and after Delivery; and the new Methods of Practice recommended by the Author.

UTERINE Hæmorrhages and Convulsions being two of the most dangerous and alarming maladies which can happen to pregnant women; I am inclined to hope, the observations contained in the two following sections will become useful; especially as they are drawn from repeated experience, in the course of several years practice. Few authors have treated professedly or practically on those subjects; for, it has been too much the custom of one, to copy and adopt the methods of another, and to recommend them from hear-say, or on the authority of his predecessors, rather than from the test of his own experience; to the great detriment of true medical knowledge.

A uterine

A uterine hæmorrhage or flooding, is a preternatural difcharge of blood from the womb, arifing from a feparation of the placenta from its interior furface, which in general, may be looked upon as its immediate caufe; but the remote caufes are various; they may proceed from external violence, as blows, falls, or the over exertion of the body in lifting heavy weights. Inflammatory fevers, the violent paffions of the mind, or whatever will preternaturally increafe the momentum of the blood on the uterine-veffels, may alfo be productive of this difcharge.

Nothing will fo much contribute to the true knowledge of uterine hæmorrhages, as due attention to the peculiar ftructure of the *placenta* and *gravid uterus,* and their attachment to each other; this will not only more clearly point out the fource from whence blood proceeds, but alfo the degree of danger to the mother and child.

The

The *placenta* may be looked upon as an apparatus or medium of intercourse, formed by nature for carrying on circulation between the mother and child : It is not only made up by one umbilical vein, and two arteries, which divide and subdivide till they become infinitely small, but also by a confiderable quantity of *cellular fubftance* every where interpofed among the ramifications of thofe veffels. This cellular part is abundantly fupplied with veffels from the uterus, but they are to be confidered as a fyftem diftinct from that of the umbilical veffels, with which they have no communication ; at leaft, that can be demonftrated ; for, the fubtileft injections have never been found to pafs into one, by filling the other ; the firft can only be injected from the uterus, the laft from the body of the fœtus.

Hence it appears, there is a two-fold circulation in the placentary mafs, and that although there is a continuation of veffels and *circulation of red blood between the uterus*

and

and placenta, there is none between the mother and child, by means of the umbilical veffels.

Indeed it has been matter of difpute, whether the ultimate branches of the placentary vein anaftomofe with thofe of the uterus, fo as to tranfmit red blood from the mother to the child ; or whether they ftrike root in the uterus, and from thence only abforb a milky fluid for the nourifhment of the fœtus, which is afterwards converted into blood by the circulating power of its heart and arteries ; and in the fame manner as blood is generated by the *chick in ovo*.

Arantius, a learned Profeffor in the univerfity of *Bologna*, I think, was the firft who denied a circulation of red blood between the mother and child, by continuation of veffels paffing from one to the other; and the rather, as he obferves that there is no kind of proportion between the innumerable branches of the placentary veffels, compared to thofe of the uterus, to render their

their *anastomosis* in the least probable:

" *Illud tandem hanc vasorum unionem minime*
" *concedi posse attestatur, quod nulla sit vasorum*
" *uteri cum innumeris umbilicalium radicibus,*
" *& capillamentis proportio, eoquo magis quod*
" *uteri vasa per matricis propriam substantiam*
" *potius sanguinem effundant, quam ad inter-*
" *nam superficiem suis osculis pertingant.*"[*]

The late celebrated Dr. *Monro*, was of the same opinion. He imagined, the extreme branches of the umbilical vein took up a lymphatic part of the blood from the uterine sinus's, in the same manner that *lacteals* absorb chyle from the cavity of the intestines.[†]

Perhaps it may be urged, that although the umbilical vein only receives a nutritious fluid from the uterus, yet the arteries must return their red blood to it, otherwise it would become redundant; but seeing

that

---

[*] *Arant.* de Human. Fœt. p. 24.
[†] *Edin.* Med. Essays, Vol. II. p. 133.

that there is a free anaſtomoſis between theſe veſſels, in the ſubſtance of the placenta; the greateſt part of that arterial blood ſuppoſed to be carried back to the uterus, is in fact, taken up by the umbilical veins, and returned to the child.* Indeed, the moſt accurate anatomiſts now ſeem to agree, that the ultimate branches both of the umbilical arteries and veins, reach the convex ſurface of the placenta, and proceed no further.

If we may compare vegetables with animals; it ſeems moſt likely, that the child in utero is at firſt nouriſhed by the ſame abſorbent power, as roots in the earth; or like *paraſite plants,* which draw their nouriſhment from that body into which they are inſerted.† Perhaps it may alſo be a probable conjecture, that the uterine veſſels, which enter the cellular ſubſtance of the placenta,

---

* According to *Rohault,* only a ſeventh part of the arterial blood is returned by the umbilical arteries to the convex ſurface of the placenta.

† Vide *Parſon's* Analogy between the propagation of animals and *vegetables.*

placenta, may there depofit a nutritious lymph, which is afterwards abforbed by the extreme branches of the umbilical vein, for the fervice of the foetus.

From this reafoning, drawn from the ftructure of the parts; a circumftance, which has often appeared unaccountable, becaufe it was imperfectly underftood, will become more obvious, viz. Why the child may furvive, in utero, for a confiderable time, and without being deprived of blood, although the mother is almoft exhaufted and brought to the point of death by an ex-ceffive lofs of that fluid; for the blood, in flooding cafes, is difcharged immediately from thofe very *veffels which fpring from the uterus*, and enter into the cellular fubftance of the placenta, and not from the extreme branches of the *funis umbilicalis* on its con-vex furface; the firft being parts peculiar to the womb, the laft proper to the child.

The

The *false chorion* invefting the exterior furface of the *placenta*, is alfo numeroufly fupplied with thofe *uterine veffels*; and it may be laid down as a practical Rule without exception, that whenever a large quantity of this tender *vafcular membrane* comes away, attended with pain and a fanguineous difcharge; it infallibly denotes a feparation of the placenta from the uterus; the patient will therefore neceffarily *mifcarry*, notwithftanding every attempt to prevent it; this reddifh flaky fubftance, being as it were, the very cement and *bond of union* between thofe two parts.

The illuftrious *Harvey* afferts, that when the mother was even extinct. and almoft ftiff with cold, he had found the umbilicial arteries beating, and the fœtus vigorous and ftrong: He alfo denies the anaftomofis of veffels between the placenta and uterus.

" *Imo vero in ejufmodi Cæfonibus, mem-*
" *brana chorio etiamnum obvolutis, fæpe re-*
S   " *peri*

"*peri (matre jam extincta & plane rigida)*
"*arterias umbilicales micantes, fœtumque ve-*
"*getum. Quare haud verum est spiritus a*
"*matre per arterias ad fœtum peringere:*
"*Nec magis verum vasa fœtus umbilicalis*
"*cum uteri vasis per Anastomosin con-*
"*jungi*.*"

A *new-born child* will live many hours
after the birth without nourishment;
for it then exists by a circulation of its
own, and being replete with blood and
juices, stands in no immediate need of additional supply; in like manner it will
continue alive for a given time in utero,
when cut off from all communication with
the mother; that is, after a separation of
the placenta; but although it there receives no red blood, it must necessarily
languish and die at last from the want of
lymph, or that nutritious something which
is essential to life; like a tender plant,
which

* *Harv*. Op. a Colleg. Medic. *Londin*. edit. p. 590.

which cannot long fubfift without the ufe of water, or refrefhing fhowers *.

Such fluxes of blood as happen after delivery, may be brought on by violent extraction of the *placenta* ; diftenfion of the uterus in twin-cafes, from a fecond child ; or by a defect of its contractive power, from a general weaknefs of the the folid fyftem.

Uterine hæmorrhages are more or lefs dangerous, in proportion as the patient is advanced in the time of pregnancy. In the firft two or three months, the embryo enjoys little more than *vegetable life* ; the veffels connecting it to the *uterus* being very fmall ; confequently, the blood is then difcharged by fuch flow and infenfible degrees, that there is generally time to fupply the lofs, by replenifhing them with nourifhing fluids, fo as to keep up the circulation.

S 2

When

* Vide, Greg. Nymman. de Vitæ Foetus in Utero.

When this is the case, the patient will fustain the lofs of a large quantity of blood, without much diminution of strength; but on the contrary, when the difcharge is great and fudden, the event is frequently fatal; and the rather if it happens in the laft months of pregnancy, when the uterine veffels are large and replete with blood.

The vaft profufion of this fluid gives fo fudden a check to the circulation, that there is not fufficient quantity returned to the heart to keep it in due motion; fo that its action either languifhes for a time, and the patient faints; or wholly ceafes, and fhe expires in a *fyncope.**

Floodings from bruifes or falls, are generally of the worft confequence; for the patient is then not only in danger fimply
from

* According to *Haller's* doctrine, the motion of the heart principally depends on the irritability of the right auricle, which is ftimulated into motion, by the influx of blood from the *vena cava*.

from the lofs of blood, but alfo from the
nature of the injury itfelf. They are alfo
extremely fallacious and fatal in the laft
months of pregnancy; for, they will frequently ceafe for a time, and remove the
appearance of danger; but as often fuddenly return, and fometimas carry her off
before there is time to effect delivery,
which is the only expedient, in fuch cafes,
that can poffibly fave her life.

When the uterus is emptied of its contents, it contracts, and gradually becomes
lefs in bulk, efpecially if the vital powers
are not much impaired by the preceding
difcharge; confequently, the current of
blood in the branches of the *hypogaftric*
and *fpermatic arteries* will meet with
refiftance, and its momentum on the
bleeding orifices of thefe veffels being confiderably diminifhed, the flooding will then
either abate or totally ceafe; fo that a dex-
terous operator will fometimes be able to do
more for the fafety of his patient by ma-

nual

nual operation, than could possibly be effected by the most skilful administration of medicines.

When any part of the placenta has been separated from the uterus, it will not again adhere, as appears after delivery; for that precise quantity of it which was disunited, is plainly pointed out, by being covered with black, coagulated blood. Hence the reason is obvious, why those hæmorrhages which go off for a time, are so extremely dangerous by their sudden return; for they do not cease because there is a re-union of divided vessels, but because the circulation languishes from profuse loss of blood, so that the patient faints; during which interval, its impulse is diminished, and the vessels being freed from their distending power, will not only gradually contract from the natural cohesion of their parts; but the blood being almost in a state of rest, will coagulate, and as it were, seal up their contracted orifices. Here

Here it is neceffary to remark that pernicious and deftructive method of giving
heating cordials or *fpirituous liquors*, with a
view to revive the patient, to which,
many have unhappily fallen victims; yet
is is ftill fo prevalent, efpecially among
the lower clafs of people, that it never
can be fufficiently difcountenanced, or its
danger too fully pointed out. Many women, during their *fainting fits*, are plentifully fupplied with warm fpiced wine or
caudle, with the addition of brandy,
which will increafe the blood's motion,
and again force open the bleeding veffels;
and thus they will alternately continue to
flood, and faint till the hour of death.
The defign of fuch proceedings may be
good, but the confequence will be fatal.

Although nothing is more difficult than
to root out prejudice from ignorant minds;
yet, he who will conform to vulgar errors
at the expence of his patient's fafety, and
is afraid to oppofe them, left his own inte-

S 4

reft

reft fhould fuffer, acts below the dignity of his profeffion, aud the principles of an honeft man.

If the moft unintelligent of mankind was afked, whether a perfon over-heated with ftrong liquor, or one half-chilled to death with cold, would bleed moft profufely, on receiving a wound in any part of his body ? furely he would reply, the former :   The cafe is fimiliar in refpect to *Uterine Hæmorrhages* ; yet fuch is the prevalence of cuftom, that the method of giving cordials, as they are called, is ftill obftinately followed, contrary to the patient's fafety, as well as reafon, and common fenfe.

Thofe who confider the origin and diftribution of the *hypogaftric* and *fpermatic arteries,* which branch off from large trunks, aud numeroufly fupply the uterus ; muft needs perceive with what rapidity the blood paffes through thofe veffels ; particularly the firft, which are

very

very large in the gravid ftare, and confequently, how foon the patient may be
exhaufted in profufe floodings, efpecially
in plethoric habits, or where the action
of the heart and arteries is increafed by
fpirituous liquors, or heating regimen*.

Under fuch circumftances, the beft cordials are thofe fluids which replenifh the
empty veffels, without heating the body;
and therefore, broths prepared from animal fubftances, jellies, and the like, are,
of all others, the fitteft to afford expeditious nourifhment; as they will foon be
affimilated, and converted into blood,
without much affiftance from the ftomach
or vital powers, which at this time are fo
much impaired.

To fubjoin particular hiftories of flooding cafes, would prove of little ufe to a
practical Reader; fince profufe difcharges
of blood happening in the laft months of
pregnancy, are generally fuch, as no medicines

* Vide *Hewfon's* Accurate Experiments on the Blood.

dicines have power to remove ; for as long as the uterus remains in a state of disten- sion, so long will its vessels continue to pour out blood, especially where a large quantity of the *placenta* is separated from it ; and therefore, it would be very unsafe to expect from medicines, what can only be brought about by speedy delivery, which produces a *mechanical change* in the structure of that organ by removing its contents.

But although this is the principal ex- pedient, and the most effectual remedy in such cases, unfortunately, it does not always secure the patient from fu- ture danger ; for the force and energy with which the womb contracts, being in proportion to the bodily strength, ra- ther than the length of time the patient has been delivered ; whenever that is greatly diminished, the flux of blood may still continue. This is the reason why a flooding before delivery sometimes occa- sions

sions the like discharge afterwards. In the several bodies which were opened, when the *Child-bed Fever* proved mortal; I had sufficient opportunity of ascertaining this fact, and constantly found that where the patient was strong, and not invaded with fever till later than usual, there the uterus was greatly diminished in bulk; but on the contrary, where she was naturally weak, or rendered so by a sudden attack of the disease; it then became inert, and was found less firm and contracted.

Puzos particularly takes notice, that when the uterus contracts imperfectly after delivery, the consequence is dangerous; and also remarks, that after the patient is delivered by turning the child; she often dies in consequence of the violence applied, or by a continuance of the discharge: he asserts, that floodings are most profuse when the labor-pains are weakest, and therefore concludes, it would be right in such cases, to procure pain artificially, by dilating the

os

os uteri, which will put the uterus into a
state of contraction, by which the child will
at last be expelled. This he calles the happy medium between natural delivery, and
that which is forced, by violently turning
the child ; and affures us, that by this method he had been extremely fuccefsful.

I remember an inftance of the good effect of this method, in a gentlewoman to
whom I was called in *York Buildings*, feveral years ago. From Sunday evening till
the Tuefday following about twelve
o'clock, at which time I was defired to vifit her, the flooding had continued profufe.

She was attended by her midwife, and
had drank plentifully of port wine, in
which a hot iron had been quenched, to
render it the more aftringent, as I fuppofe : Her afpect was death-like, fhe
frequently fainted ; her pulfe was almoft
imperceptible, and fhe feemed finking very
faft.   The

The full time of reckoning was expired; but as her strength was much exhausted, the labor-pains were inconsiderable, and the os uteri but little dilated. I immediately broke the membranes, that the resistance to the languid contraction of the uterus might be less, and supplied her with *veal broth*, made moderately strong, but without salt or spices: Of this nourishing fluid, given cold, she swallowed a tea-cupful, or as much as her stomach would bear, every quarter of an hour, having taken nothing of the like kind before. The cold, fresh air, was also freely admitted into her chamber, which seemed to give her new life; for she found her strength and spirits, as well as her pains, increase very fast; and by dilating the os uteri, they at last became so strong, as to effect the birth before evening, without the danger of turning the child, which, notwithstanding the vast discharge of blood, was born *vigorous* and *strong*; agreeable to what I have remarked elsewhere.

A

A curious example of the efficacy and reficient quality of nourishing fluids in sustaining life and restoring strength, even when the assimilating powers of body were not sufficient to convert them into blood, is mentioned by *Lower* in his book De Corde, viz.* *Adolescenti sedecim annos nato cum magna sanguinis copia (qua de causa non refert) perbiduam continuo erumperet, neque medicamentis aut arte ulla cohiberi potuit; jusculis cum reficere & recreare amici & astantes curarunt; cumque ea valde avide expeteret atque assumeret, fluxus subinde concitatior quoque factus est, & tandem res eo devenit, ut massa sanguinis fere tota emissa, quicquid jam efflueret, dilutum & pallidum, sanguinis neque naturam neque speciem pre se ferret, ipsi jusculo quod toties hauserat quam sanguini similius: Atque eadem forma per diem unum aut alterum duravit hic aequeus fluxus, constante interim cordi motu suo, donec fluxa demum consopito juvenis paulatim integræ saluti restitutus est, & exinde in virum robustum & quadratum accrevit.*

In

* De Corde, Cap ii. p. 63.

In order to know whether *topical applications*, *medicines*, or *manual operation*, will moft effectually relieve the patient in uterine hæmorrhages; their various caufes fhould be attentively confidered, with the feveral circumftances of the cafe, alfo her habit of body, and the different ftate of the uterus before and after delivery.

In thofe fluxes of blood which happen during labor, or at the full expiration of pregnancy, it will be proper to break the membranes, for the uterus will contract after the difcharge of the waters, and the flooding will therefore be diminifhed : particularly as the bleeding veffels will then be brought into contact with the child, as it were, by comprefs and bandage. But as this method only procures relief to a certain degree, if the fymptoms become urgent and the labor does not quickly advance, the patient ought to be delivered as foon as poffible.

When

When the child's head shuts up the os uteri, the patient may continue losing blood profusely into the cavity of the womb, although none externally appears ; this is to be feared when her pulse sinks, attended with great faintness and sudden loss of strength, without any evident cause ; and will best be known by pressing up the head in the absence of the labor-pains, so as to let the confined blood escape. Such cases are extremely dangerous and fallacious, where the operator is not sufficiently upon his guard.

Sometimes the *placenta* has been found presenting loose at the os uteri, or adhering to that part ; in both cases, especially the first, a flooding will happen, attended with great danger ; and therefore will require speedy delivery, which may be effected either by the *long double-curv'd forceps*, or turning the child, as appears most eligible from different circumstances ; for as the whole placentary mass is separated from the womb, the least delay would prove fatal to the patient.

Those

Thofe hæmorrhages which happen where the child has long been dead in utero, are alfo attended with imminent danger ; becaufe, as there is then no longer any circulation in the *placenta*, the cafe will be nearly the fame as when it prefented loofe, although it does not appear fo alarming.

January the 20th, 1765, I was fent for to Mrs. G—, a gentlewoman in *Piccadilly*, who was feized with a flux of blood from the uterus, near the full time of pregnancy ; as it was not profufe, and her ftrength and fpirits were good, I waited for fome hours in expectation of ftronger pains, but as the difcharge feemed to go off, and fhe was difpofed to fleep, I left her and defired to be called if it returned with violence, or when the pains became ftronger. When I vifited the next day, they were inconfiderable, and, the os uteri was very little dilated ; but though fhe continued to lofe blood, her ftrength feemed little impaired :

T   paired :

paired :   In this situation she remained several days, during which, she took a decoction of *bark*, with *tinct. rosar. r.* and a few drops of *tinct. thebaic.*

At last the discharge became intolerably putrid, and was soon followed by a large secretion of milk, which flowed from her breasts by the slightest pressure : The flooding now began to increase very much ; she grew weak and faint, and certainly would soon have sunk under the discharge, had she not speedily been delivered.

The child had been dead several days before the secretion of milk, which began as soon as the *placenta* was separated from the womb ; for then the hæmorrhage was observed to increase.   The same circumstance may happen when the fœtus in utero is weak, and the absorbing power of the *placenta* from thence in part destroyed ; agreeable to what is laid down by *Hippocrates* in his Aphor. *viz. Mulieri in utero gerenti,*

renti, si multum lactis ex mammis fluxerit, infir-
mum fœtum significat. *

In ftrong habits, where the uterine fibres
are tenfe, the flooding generally ftops, and
the placenta is eafily excluded foon after
delivery ; but on the contrary, when the
patient is very weak, much longer time is
then required for its coming away ; and if
it fhould be unwarily extracted before the
uterus has had fufficient time to contract,
or where it afterwards continues loofe and
inactive; a mortal hæmorrhage may chance
to enfue. Indeed it fometimes happens that
the lofs of bloo d is profufe, even after delivery, where the placenta remains ; under
which circumftance it may be proper immediately to take it away : Here the action
of the uterus is fo extremely languid, that
it has not power either to expel the placenta, or large quantity of coagulated blood
collected in its cavity : A fatal inftance of

T 2   this

* Sect. v. Aphor. 52.

this kind occurred to me in the year 1770, in the cafe of Mrs. W——— near Weft-minfter-Bridge, to whom I was called about an hour and a half after fhe had been delivered by her midwife.

The internal ufe of medicines, as far as I have obferved, ought never folely to be depended upon in fuch cafes ; for although they may afford fome relief in a certain time ; the patient would generally bleed to death before they could have fufficient effect ; and therefore, immediate recourfe muft be had to topical applications, fuch as *oxycrate* or *fharp vinegar*, in which thick linen compreffes have been dipped, and which are to be applied cold to the belly and loins, and renewed as foon as they grow warm, otherwife they will relax rather than conftringe.

Gentle preffure on the belly, by means of a broad circular roller, will alfo prove of fervice, by refifting the too rapid courfe

of

of the blood through the uterus, and also by affisting its languid contraction.

The patient fhould be kept very *cool*, and if neceffary, *expofed to cold air, even in the midft of winter, by opening doors and windows,* fo as to let it be equally diffufed round her chamber; her drinks fhould be given *cold*, and acidulated with lemon juice or mineral acids; and if ever the ufe of *ftyptics* can prove of fervice, perhaps it may be here; where the uterus, although empty, has not the power of being reftored to its former ftate. I have found a ftrong *decoction of bark* and *elixir of vitriol*, with a fmall quantity of tincture of cinnamon to make it grateful, more efficacious than any thing I have feen tried.

The form may be varied at difcretion, and if neceffary, the extract may be added, viz.

℞

Decoct. Peruv. Cort. ℥ *i*
Extract. ejufd. moll. ℈ *i*

T 3

Tinct

Tinct. Rosar. rub. ℨ*ſs*

—— *Cinn.* ℨ *iij*

Confect. Alkerm. ℨ *j fiat hauſtus pro re nata ex-hibendus.*

When the diſcharge is attended with much pain or irritation of the uterus; five or more drops of *thebaic tincture* may be joined with each draught; or, what will produce its effect with more certainty, a liberal doſe of the *pil. e ſtyrace,* or *ex-tract. thebaic.* The firſt may be given from two to ſix grains or more, and the laſt from half a grain, to a grain and half, which may be repeated as occaſion requires; eſpecially, where the habit is not plethoric, and when the ſymptoms are extremely urgent.

If all thoſe methods fail, and the patient is in imminent danger; the *aqua aluminoſa batean.* or a weak ſolution of *colcothar of vitriol,* injected into the cavity of the uterus as a ſtyptic, will probably reſtrain the diſcharge; by coming into immediate contact

with

with the orifices of the bleeding veffels; but thofe remedies are only applicable after delivery, when it is empty and uncontracted.

My worthy and accomplifhed friend Dr. *Gordon*, a native of Denmark, and affiftant to the Profeffor of Midwifery at *Copenhagen*, who attended my Lectures laft winter, informed me, that agreeable to the above hints, they had injected *cold water* into the *uterus*, in feveral cafes of profufe flooding, with the moft defirable fuccefs, and without the leaft danger, or fubfequent bad fymptoms. *Saxtorph* alfo recommends oxycrate to be injected into the *womb* in uterine hæmorrhages, after delivery, and mentions feveral cafes in which it fucceeded after every other method had failed.[*]

Hoffman tells us, he fucceeded in ftopping a profufe *uterine hæmorrhage*, which had withftood every other method, by paffing up *pledgets of lint*, dipped in a folution of

T 4   *colcothar*

---

[*] Vide, *Acta Societatis Medicæ Haunienfis.*

colcothar of vitriol, as high into the vagina
as poffible ; and fince the patient afterwards
conceived, and had a happy delivery, he obferves that the functions of the uterus were
not in the leaft injured by the ftyptic power
of this application.

M. Leroux, furgeon to the General Hofpital at *Dijon* in France, two years ago,
publifhed a Treatife profeffedly on *Uterine
Hæmorrhages*, with which he honored me
as a Prefent ; he particularly mentions the
method laid down by Hoffman, as well as
thofe which I have recommended.

Levret hit upon a very odd, but ingenious
expedient in ftopping a violent flooding
after delivery, which otherwife would foon
have proved fatal : He introduced a piece
of *ice* into the uterus, which being ftruck
with fudden chill, immediately contracted
and put a ftop to the hæmorrhage.

The moft extraordinary inftance of a
flux of blood from the womb, which I
have ever heard of, fell under the obfervation of the late Dr. *Cole*, who, fome
years

years ago, practised midwifery in *London* with great reputation : On opening the body, the whole surface of the *placenta* was found adhering to the uterus ; but a great part of the *false chorion* investing the membranous bag which contains the child, was separated from it ; and consequently, an infinite number of those vessels with which it is supplied from the uterus, being torn asunder, the effusion of blood was so great as to become mortal. From what cause this accident was brought on I have not been able to inform myself. Those slight discharges, which sometimes go off, and allow the patient to proceed her full period of gestation, have been imputed to loss of blood from the *false chorion* of the bag only, and not to a separation of the *placenta* itself ; and indeed notwithstanding what has already been said, I am still inclined to think so ; for whenever any part of the last is dis-united from the uterus, there is the greatest reason

to

to fuppofe it will never again adhere, although *Noortwyk*, in his hiftory of the gravid uterus, has afferted the contrary.*

Some floodings have occurred, attended with very uncommon circumftances. The celebrated *Albinus* mentions a cafe, where only the central part of the placenta being loofened, a large quantity of coagulated blood was lodged between it and the womb, as it were in a bag; and confequently not a drop was externally difcharged, fo as to foretel the danger.

Sometimes blood has been found to proceed from the vagina; and at other times from a rupture of veffels on the concave furface of the placenta, or even in the funis itfelf, which muft neceffarily foon prove fatal to the child, but will not proportionably endanger the mother. The preternatural fhortnefs of the funis, or it being twifted round the child's neck, have alfo been fuppofed to bring on flooding; for if

it

* *Noortwyk* de Uter. Gravid. p. 28.

it then moves powerfully, the placenta may be torn from the uterus.

Whatever fubjects the body to violent motion, or agitates the mind, fhould be carefully avoided; for it has already been fhewn in treating of *Child-bed Fever*, at page 88, how much the force of the circulating blood on its veffels is increafed by mufcular motion. Coughing, fneezing, a tenefmus, or other efforts which lay ftrefs on the womb, all tend, in degree, to deftroy its union with the contained parts; efpecially, immoderate exercife in the laft months of pregnancy, when the child is large and ponderous.

Paffions of the mind, efpecially fudden terror, have alfo frequently been known to produce this diforder; a very remarkable inftance of which is related by *Salmuth*, as follows* :

Archi-

* *Salm.* Obfer. Med. Cent. x. 3. xli

Archiatri Anhaltini D. S. K. conjunx puer-
pera lactat infantem sub noctem.   Per jocum a
mulieribus quibusdam ex convivio domum ten-
dentibus fores & fenestræ nimis impetuose pul-
santur.   Illa hinc admodum perterrita, totoq.
corpore contremiscente, repente excitatur proflu-
vium mensium, in annum integrum perdurans,
& adeo quidem copiosum, ut per stragula etiam
deflueret, atque ex eo ipsa tandem moreretur.

Some years ago, I was desired to visit
a gentlewoman near *Berkley-Square,* who
was seized with flooding from over-
hasty extraction of the *placenta,* by which
she was reduced to the last degree of
weakness: I desired she might be kept
extremely quiet, and supplied with frequent nourishment; I also directed a
mixture with *tincture of roses* and soft extract of *bark, &c.* of which she took two
spoonful as often as her stomach could bear:
In a short time she found herself much
recovered, but towards morning, by only
turning herself hastily in bed, the discharge
im-

immediately returned in great profusion.
I was again called, and found her to all
appearance at the point of death ; but by
the application of thick compresses dipped
in cold vinegar, to her belly and loins,
with the same methods as before, she at
last perfectly recovered.

Excessive anger, or sudden fear produce
spasm, or contraction of the vascular system, by which blood is driven from the
surface to the centre of the body ; as
is evident from paleness of the face, which
is instantly followed by throbbing and
palpitation at heart ; soon after, the countenance becomes florid, from re-action
of the heart, which throws out blood
to the surface again. Hence, during
the spasm, the venous blood is violently
driven to the right auricle, and the velocity of the arterial blood discharged from
the left ventricle into the *aorta descendens*
will therefore be considerably increased,
and consequently, that circulating through
the

the arteries of the womb, from which the placenta may be forced away, and hæmorrhage ensue.

This tumult in the body is produced by nervous influence which affects it like a flight electric shock ; accordingly, women of delicate constitutions, whose nervous system is extremely irritable, are, of all others, the most subject to those complaints ; I have likewise observed, in such habits where the patient was not pregnant, and the *uterus*, therefore, not susceptible of the impression ; that pain in the bowels or diarrhœa have often been brought on, and sometimes a dangerous fever ; particularly when the former symptoms did not occur.

Bleeding and *styptics*, with the liberal use of *opium*, and application of *ligatures* to the extremities of the body, are the remedies which have been principally depended upon, for the cure of *uterine hæmorrhages* ; and therefore it will be necessary to examine their effects.   By

By attending to the circulation, it is evident, that *bleeding* can seldom be proper, except in the beginning of thofe floodings which happen before delivery; or when they arife from plethora; an inflammatory fever, or external violence. Sometimes, indeed, if the patient fhould be threatened with this malady, after violent furprize, it may alfo be requifite; but as in general, weakly, hyfterical women, who have been obferved to bear the lofs of blood with inconvenience, are the ofteneft thus affected, it fhould be directed with great caution; efpecially, as *opiates* and the *warm bath* will anfwer much better, by diffolving the fpafm, and foothing the nerves into a ftate of tranquillity.

Befides; it has been proved that the contraction of the uterus after delivery, upon which the abatement of this difcharge chiefly depends, will be in proportion to the bodily ftrength; and therefore, an additional lofs of blood from the arm at that period,

period, would farther endanger the patient, both by diminifhing the action of the womb, and giving fo fudden a check to the circulation, as might occafion dangerous faintings, or perhaps a mortal fyncope.

Styptic medicines have been fuppofed to reftrain internal hæmorrhages, by entering the blood, and conftringing the orifices of the bleeding veffels ; and therefore are accounted falutary, and efficacious in fuch complaints ; but with what foundation, I appeal to common experience.

If ftyptics produce their effect by contracting the veffels, they muft alfo increafe their action on the contained blood ; for it will be nearly the fame thing, with refpect to the velocity of the blood ; whether its veffels are preternaturally filled, when their diameters remain the fame as before, or whether their diameters are preternaturally leffened, when their quantity of blood is the fame ; or in other words,

words, *when the same quantity of blood is contained in a narrower space, its veffels will from thence become fuller.* For example ; if a certain quantity of any fluid is forced through two flexible tubes of different diameters, but of the fame length, and in the fame given time ; its velocity in the fmalleft tube will neceffarily be greater than in the other : Hence it becomes manifeft, that if ftyptic or aftringent medicines act by contracting the orifices of the bleeding veffels, they muft alfo act univerfally on the vafcular fyftem ; and if fo, by leffening the diameters of the feveral veffels, their action on the contained blood will be increafed, which muft alfo neceffarily increafe the flooding.

If it fhould be alledged that they operate by coagulating the blood, and not by bracing its veffels ; or that, like *opium*, they produce their effects by mediation of the nerves of the ftomach, without entering the blood at all ; it is to be remarked, that

U   whatever

whatever thickens the blood, will, moſt probably, alſo conſtringe its veſſels. In ſhort, by what means ſoever they affect the habit; it is plain that an hæmorrhage can only be ſtopped either by ſuch things as contract the ruptured veſſels, or diminiſh the force of the fluid paſſing through them. The firſt of theſe effects has already been conſidered ; and the laſt muſt be denied, ſince what occaſions *thirſt and fever,* as ſtyptics do, cannot properly be ſaid to leſſen the circulating power, but increaſe it.

No wonder then that *Hoffman* aſſerts, he has often ſeen Uterine Hæmorrhages increaſed by ſtyptics, but alſo obſtinate complaints of the chronic kind, ſuch as cachexy, dropſy, or hectic fever, brought on by their prepoſterous uſe. Agreeable to what is advanced by that excellent practical phyſician, I have ſeldom ever known the *pulv. ſtyp. tinct. ſaturnin.* or other powerful aſtringents, given in ſuch caſes, without an increaſe of the hæmorrhage, or ſome other

bad

bad effect : That they will generally render the body coſtive, and often create great thirſt, head-ach, and other febrile ſymptoms, is certain ; but the chronical complaints, with which they are charged, were more probably owing to the profuſe loſs of blood happening at the time they were adminiſtered, than to the ſubſequent injurious qualities of thoſe medicines : However, the following inſtance, as well as ſeveral others, which it would here be unneceſſary to mention, will ſhew that they are not void of danger, and therefore, ought to be directed with the utmoſt caution.

In the year 1770, a lady in *Stanhope-Street, May-Fair,* of a very delicate, valetudinary habit, had been long ſubject to the *fluor albus,* as well as an immoderate flux of menſes at undue periods, which had very much reduced her ſtrength : By the advice of an eminent phyſician, ſhe took *ſacch. ſaturn.* in a bolus, twice a-day, and continued it upwards of a week ; but did not find that

it either reftrained the difcharge, or had any
good effect refpecting her bodily ftrength ;
on the contrary, it at laft brought on an obftinate conftipation of the bowels, attended
with fuch racking, colic pains, and oppreffion at ftomach, as obliged her to keep her
body almoft double.   Being defired to vifit
her, I directed draughts with *manna* and *ol.*
amygd. with *emollient clyfters,* and the *warm.*
bath ; fhe alfo drank warm veal broth by
intervals.   After two or three lax motions,
fhe was much eafier ; but as the forenefs of
her bowels continued, fhe took an emulfion
with *fperm. ceti,* for a few days, which removed it ; and afterwards, by the ufe of
a ftrong decoction of *bark,* with an *injection*
and the chalybeate waters, fhe was entirely
freed from the fluor albus and all her other
complaints.

Internal hæmorrhages will often at laft
fpontaneoufly ceafe, without the affiftance
of any medicines whatever, efpecially when
profufe ; for as the power of the heart on
the

the circulating blood will then be greatly diminifhed, its momentum on the bleeding veffels will be confiderably lefs ; and it has already been remarked, that they will naturally contract when freed from their diftending power. Hence there is reafon to think that the ceffation of this difcharge, after the exhibition of ftyptics, is not owing to fuch medicines, but to a diminution of the circulating force from lofs of ftrength.

Inftead therefore of bracing the folids, it would be more proper to recur to the ufe of things which have a power to relax, and as it were, fufpend their action : Such medicines are called *fedatives*, and are fuppofed not only to leffen the circulating force, but produce a more equal diftribution of blood, and occafion the derivation of a larger quantity from the interior veffels to the bodily furface. Hence the uterine arteries will be relieved from their diftenfion, and the flux of blood proceeding from thence will confequently be lefs. To this

U 3

end,

end, the fourth part of a grain of *emetic tartar* may be given, and repeated by due intervals, so as only to excite nausea, without vomiting; also *saline draughts*, with *nitre*; or the *sal sedativ. of Hombergh*, from five grains to a scruple. In what manner such medicines operate, is difficult to determine; but that they often have a salutary effect, is evident from experience.

How far the effect of *opiates* may be depended upon, or under what circumstances they are pernicious in flooding cases, it will next be necessary to enquire. From some experiments made by Dr. *Alston* on frogs, it appears, that *opium* taken internally, will for a time, retard the blood's motion, by diminishing the vital power of the heart; and this circumstance, so far as it regards those small aquatic animals, is still further confirmed by that incomparable Physiologist the late Dr. *Whytt*: Such experiments are pleasing and curious, but the inferences arising from them, when applied to the

the human body, are not so conclusive and satisfactory, as they at first appear; for many substances which produce a mortal effect on one species of animals, are not found injurious to another; and the same animal is very differently affected by the same thing at different times. Would it not therefore, be a more certain way to determine the effects of *opium* on human bodies, by attending particularly to its operation, on such bodies only?

In several cases, where it was necessary to direct *opiates* for women, at the beginning of labor, to remove their unprofitable pains and procure sleep, I have been surprised to find they had a very contrary effect, and that from thence the pains were evidently much increased.

Dr. *Young*, who wrote professedly on *opium*, is the only author I know, that takes notice of the same thing. His observations are founded on long and extensive experience, which he confesses often contradicted the

U 4 opinion

opinions he had adopted from theory ; consequently he frequently changed his methods of practice ; and it is much to be wished that an example so laudable, was more universally followed. Indeed, the greatest part of his book appears to be a true history of the effects of this extraordinary medicine, and as he rather relates what he saw, than what he expected to see, his authority is more to be regarded.

Baron Haller, in his dissertation on the irritable parts of animals, observes ; that although *opium* destroys the peristaltic motion of the intestines, and irritability of the body in general, it leaves the heart unimpaired. What I have seen of its effects on the human body, exactly corresponds with this remark ; for though it may suspend some of the secretions, it rather, at first, *quickens the blood's motion,* than retards it. For instance, a moderate dose will strengthen and inlarge the pulse, the eyes sparkle, the countenance

becomes

becomes florid, and a heat and itching of the ſkin ſucceeds; but what appears moſt extraordinary, thoſe pains which have ſometimes been increaſed by it, in a ſmall quantity, were ſpeedily removed by giving a more liberal doſe. In ſhort, I have clearly ſeen internal hæmorrhages rather increaſed than leſſened by its uſe; and therefore, think it ought not to be given, except in caſes of neceſſity, as its effects are evidently ſimilar to thoſe of volatile medicines, or ſtrong cordials.

In the beginning of floodings which ariſe from plethora, fever, or external violence, eſpecially where the *pulſe is hard*, and the ſkin dry; both *opiates* and *ſtyptics* are highly pernicious. *Bleeding*, *laxatives*, and *ſpare diet*, with cooling regimen, are beſt adapted to anſwer the intention of cure. The judicious *Hoffman*, therefore, with great reaſon, directs the liberal uſe of *ſpring water* with *ſpirits of vitriol* and *ſyrup of red poppies*, as a medicine more

ſalutary

salutary than the moſt boaſted ſpecifics : On the contrary, in the decline of thoſe diſ-charges, where the *pulſe is weak*, and the *circulation languid*, from loſs of blood, it will be proper to keep the patient in a horizontal poſition, leſt ſhe ſhould faint. A *ſtrong infuſion of bark*, and even cordial medicines may alſo be adminiſtered, eſpe-cially after delivery, where there is al-ways leſs danger of the flooding's return ; the reſiſtance to the womb's contraction being then taken away.   Nouriſhment ſhould be given often, and in ſmall quanti-ties, that the empty veſſels may be reple-niſhed by degrees ; otherwiſe, as the ſtomach is weak, and aſſimilating powers of the body much impaired, the patient will be apt to fall into *dropſy, conſumption*, or *hectic fever*.

The ancients applied *ligatures* to the infe-rior extremities, for the relief of uterine hæmorrhages ; from which it may be con-cluded, they knew more of the circulation than

than has been imagined ; for it is plain they
had recourfe to this method, with a view to
retard the venous blood in its return to the
heart, and confequently to abate the circulating force. But this practice does not
feem juft, neither is it found experimentally ufeful ; but on the contrary, dangerous and irrational.

Let us fuppofe, for inftance, that a co-
lumn of blood is driven down the *aorta defcendens*, by the action of the heart, and that
it is diftributed to the lower extremities, by
the divifion and fubdivifions of the *iliac arte-
rics*, from which the *uterus* at laft receives its
blood. The extreme branches of all thefe
arteries have correfponding veins, which
take up their blood by *anaftomofis*, and after
uniting and re-uniting, they form the *vena
cava* inferior, or one large trunk, which
returns blood from the inferior parts of the
body, to the right auricle of the heart ; if
therefore, from any compreffion of thofe
veins, the reflux of their blood is prevented,
they

they cannot then freely receive it from the arteries ; confequently, the *hypogaftrics* and *fpermatics* which fupply the *uterus* with blood will become over-charged and diftended, and the patient will flood more abundantly ; as the following ingenious experiment will clearly demonftrate.

Dr. *Hamilton* of *Edinburgh*, being called to a young woman who had labored under obftructed menfes for near feven months, from catching cold ; and finding that various remedies had been tried in vain, directed compreffes to be applied tight upon the *crural arteries*, by means of a tourniquet, which after remaining about twenty minutes, rendered the pulfe quicker ; in half an hour, fhe began to perceive a fenfe of weight and fulnefs in the region of the uterus, and in an hour and a half after the firft application of the ligatures, the menfes began to flow.

If it fhould be alledged, that the effect here produced, was owing to compreffion of

the

the *arteries*, and not the *veins* ; it may be re-
plied, that the means made ufe of to comprefs the firft, muft neceffarily have the
fame effect on the other. But fetting this
reafoning afide ; if fimple preffure on the
crural arteries has been known to bring on
menfes, after long obftruction, by impeding
the direct courfe of their blood, and throwing
a larger quantity on the *uterine veffels* ; fo
would the fame degree of preffure when applied to the *veins* themfelves ; which may
be looked upon as fo many reflected arteries,
void of pulfation, becaufe of their diftance
from the heart, which cannot extend its
influence beyond the *anaftomofes* of thefe
two orders of veffels.

Having laid before the Reader fuch general remedies as have been thought moft
conducive to the relief of that dangerous
malady under confideration ; and pointed out the pernicious tendency of a heating regimen, or the exhibition of cordial medicines ; I fhall now endeavour

to

to shew the good effect of a *contrary method*, both as supported by reason, and experience; at the same time confessing, that the perusal of Dr. *Stevenson*'s ingenious Essay on the effects of heat and cold on human bodies*, and afterwards, what I had read in the Commentaries of the celebrated *Baron Van Swieten*, in some measure, first suggested to me the propriety and expediency of such practice. The first of those authors has very sensibly refuted the absurd doctrine of *derivation* and *revulsion*; and shews that *pediluvium*, or application of warm water to the feet, the effect of which was supposed to depend upon those principles, is owing to a cause directly contrary to that hitherto assigned; as the following experiment will clearly evince.

Dr. *Stevenson* caused two youths to put their legs in warm water, and whilst they continued there, he counted their pulses by a watch measuring seconds, according to the

* Edinburgh Medical Essays, vol. vi. p. 8.

the different degrees of heat in the water, which was gradually increafed and applied from time to time : At eight o'clock in the evening, the pulfe of the firft beat fixty-fix, and that of the fecond eighty-four. As the heat was increafed, they began to breathe quicker, their countenance became florid, the veins of the face and hands were much diftended, and the pulfe increafed in proportion ; in the firft, it beat eighty, and in the fecond, ninety-eight ftrokes in a minute. In the above experiment, both their pulfes, which in the beginning, were foft and fmall, became full and hard ; and not only the parts immerfed in water, but the whole body was fwelled : The pulfes of the wrifts and temples alfo beat fuller and quicker, as well as thofe arteries derived from the *aorta defcendens* ; and confequently, there could be no *revulfion.* The legs being then removed out of the warm water ; in about half an hour's time, all the above fymptoms of fulnefs went off,

off, and the pulfe in each gradually returned to its former ftate.

From thefe premifes, the Doctor, with reafon concludes, that the blood paffing through the veffels of the legs, being heated by the *pediluvium*, imparts its additional warmth to the general mafs ; which being rarefied, takes up larger fpace in the veffels, and circulates with more rapidity than before ; and thus every part of the body is affected with a fenfe of fulnefs. Hence, he infers the great danger of this application in *hæmorrhages* from the nofe or lungs, or in diforders of the head or breaft, arifing from plenitude ; cafes where it was often formerly applied, and muft as often have been pernicious to the patient. What is ancient or modern, is not therefore right or wrong ; though this is not the only inftance where things, however prepofterous and abfurd, have derived fuch fanction from antiquity, as to render them the ftandard of future practice.

Van

Van Swieten, in treating of the diseases of virgins, expresses himself in the following manner :

Cum autem pedes & crura ab iliacis arteriis externis sua vasa accipiant, uterus ab hypogastricis non tandem, sed ab iliacis externis etiam & variis inter se anastomosibus communicent (uti in tabulis Euftachianis (1) *videri potest) facile patet, quare, per balnea laxatis pedum vasis, & dein per frictiones accelerato motu in iisdem, major copia sanguinis derivetur versus aortum, ubi in iliacas dividitur, adeoque & magis tunc urgeantur uter vasa ; sicque sperari possis, illorum extrema ita dilatari posse, et menstruum fluorem dimittant.*

Simul notandum est, practicis observatis constare, calorem pedum prodesse menstruantibus ; frigus autem nocere ; imo quandoque subito menstrua supprimi, si admodum frigescant pedes ; quod sæpius observavi ; præcipue si pavimento marmoreo frigido pedibus insistant diu. Solent enim ab hac causa sola, contractis spasmodice intestinis,

X   *dolores*

(1) **Tab.** xiii.

dolores colici oriri molestissimi, in quibus magnum levamen sentitur, si pedes incaluerint, imprimis per frictiones. Omnia enim abdominis viscera male afficiuntur, dum pedes intensè frigent ; adeoque mirum non est, & uteri vasa stringi, sicque supprimi, fluorem menstruum..

The experiment mentioned by the first author, is a clear and satisfactory illustration of the effect of *heat* on the human body ; and the practical observations of the latter, as appears by the above quotation, as sufficiently demonstrate the action of *cold*, in constringing the vessels of the uterus, and suppressing the menses, even when applied to the feet only ; from whence I would propose the following question ; *viz.* If the *topical application of cold* to the feet, has been found to put an immediate stop to an habitual discharge of blood from the uterus, in opposition to the powerful efforts of nature ; is there not the greatest reason to believe, that the same application would prove singularly efficacious,

efficacious, either in reftraining, or totally taking away that *hæmorrhage* from the womb which is preternatural ?

Heat not only relaxes the folids and diffolves the fluids, as may be feen by its effects on thofe animal fubftances, called jellies and glue, but alfo rarefies the air contained in the body, by which the whole mafs will be expanded ; and by taking up more fpace in the veffels, their diameters will be enlarged, which will lay additional ftrefs upon the folid fyftem ; fo that the effects of rarefaction and plethora, pro tempore, will be the fame. *Cold*, on the contrary, conden-fes air, and confirms the blood's texture, for even the hardeft metals, as appears by the *pyrometer*, are contracted, or expanded according to the degrees of heat or cold applied.

From thefe circumftances, but chiefly from *repeated experience*, I would infer that the application of *intenfe cold* to the body, is more to be depended upon, and will produce more falutary effects in *uterine hæmor-rhages*, than any thing elfe which can be devifed ; although I forefee an objection, which I could wifh to obviate before I go farther.   As cold affects the body by contracting the folids, and repelling blood to the interior parts ; it may be faid that its action will be equally pernicious with that of *ftyptics* : The fact feems to be this ; when the body is heated, the circulating power is increafed, and the blood is rarefied and rendered more fluid, but its veffels being dilated, if they at laft give way, will then difcharge their contents more freely ; but when it is fuddenly chilled, although the application of *cold* may contract and leffen the capacity of its veffels ; it condenfes the blood at the fame time, fo that in effect, they will not become fuller than before ; befides, as I have always obferved, that the flux of blood abated in proportion to the degree of cold ; experience, which ought to fuperfede all theory,

fhews

shews that the effect of cold in condensing the fluids, is more than equal to its power in contracting the folids; or at leaft, that the danger already hinted is not to be feared.

Floodings which are attended with frequent and long continued *fainting fits,* often prove mortal; yet I have obferved in fome of thofe where the pulfe was weak and intermitting, and who were apparently finking very faft; that by frequently admitting frefh, cold air, they recovered, as if infpired with new life. This does not feem difficult to account for, as the heart has not power to propel its blood through the pulmonary arteries, till the lungs are fufficiently blown up with cold air; which, on account of its greater gravity, is much fitter for the purpofes of refpiration, than the inelaftic, confined atmofphere of a warm bed chamber.

In *Auguft,* 1773, I received a letter from a gentleman at Kirby-Londfdale, in Weftmoreland, of which the following is an ab-

X 3   ftract.

ſtract. "I had lately an opportunity of ſeeing the good effects of *cold* in a flooding after delivery ; the particulars of which are as follows. About a month ago, I was called to a woman in labor with her fifth child, at a village a few miles from this town : The labor was natural, and in a ſhort time the placenta came away with eaſe. About half an hour after, I took a walk in the fields, but was called in great haſte, and at my return found her fainting and flooding very profuſely. On enquiry, I was informed the women had given her a large quantity of ſpirits, to which I imputed the diſcharge. I threw open the door and windows of the room, for the free admiſſion of air, *and gave her cold water plentifully to drink* ; by means of which the flooding almoſt immediately abated without any return."

A gentleman who practices midwifery in London communicated to me the follow-ing caſe :

November

November the 11th, 1773, a patient of mine was feized with a profufe flooding and fainting, about half an hour after delivery: To the beft of my knowledge, fhe loft about *three pints of blood.* I immediately let in cold frefh air upon her, by opening the doors and windows ; *and gave her two glaffes of cold water to drink ;* having no vinegar at hand, I applied thick cloths, dipped in cold water, round her loins, over the lower part of the abdomen, and to the vagina : The good effect was evident, for the flooding very foon ceafed ; in about twenty minutes the patient became fenfible, and in a voice fcarcely to be underftood, defired fhe might be covered with cloaths, for fhe was dying ; as fhe feemed to be very cold, and was in a kind of fhivering-fit, I complied with her requeft, but foon found my error in fo doing ; for when fhe became warm, the flooding returned, which obliged me to have recourfe to my former method, and to apply cloths wetted with vinegar, which by this time

X 4

was

was procured; in confequence of which, the difcharge of blood again abated in a very fhort time, and my patient happily recovered without any relapfe.

Every one who breathes with difficulty, can tell from his own experience, what vaft relief he finds in going from a hot room, where the air is too much rarefied, into one much cooler, where it is more elaftic and pure.   The frequency of a natural pulfe to the act of refpiration, is in general as *two to three* ; and the laft is found to have a very fenfible effect on the firft, both as to its ftrength and quicknefs.   Befides, as a confiderable part of the whole mafs of blood is continually paffing through the lungs ; fucceffive draughts of that *cold fluid,* conftantly applied to their interior furface, will contribute greatly to cool and condenfe it ; as nothing but the membranous expanfion of air veffels is interpofed ; and as air in the blood, will, by alternate changes always

always remain in *equilibrio* with that of the common atmosphere.

From such a rarefaction of air, the vessels of animals placed in the exhausted receiver of an air-pump, will swell and even burst; and upon the same principle, periodical pains, and fluxes of blood sometimes happen at full and new moon, when the atmospherical pressure on the surface of the body is greatly diminished. Those of delicate habits, like so many *living barometers*, feel the influence of the same cause, and become weather-wise, on the approach of high winds or sudden falls of rain.

According to *Arbuthnot*, the internal surface of the lungs is greater in its extent, than all that part of the skin exposed to air; and therefore, the large quantity of this fluid received by inspiration, added to that externally applied to the body, will have very great effect in condensing the mass of blood, and reducing it into a smaller space,

so

fo as to leffen the diftenfion of its veffels; and confequently, will not only tend to fecure the patient from danger of a fyncope, but will alfo abate the flooding.

Next to the free and unlimited ufe of *cold air*, with the application of compreffes dipped in cold vinegar, to the belly and loins; I have often, according to the practice of *Hoffman*, directed large and repeated draughts of *fpring water*, with remarkable good fuccefs; for, out of *upwards of three thoufand women* delivered in the *Weftminfter Lying-In-Hofpital*, feveral of whom were feized with floodings, both before and after delivery, only two of them failed under this treatment; as far as it was prudent to truft to it, or any other means, *independent of delivery itfelf.*

When the patient is very weak and much exhaufted, beef-water or weak broth taken cold, will be more proper than water; and where the laft is directed, it will be neceffary to tincture it with *fyrup of red*

red poppies, or fomething of the like kind,
to give it a medicinal appearance, which
will render it more acceptable : But, if
notwithftanding, the flooding becomes fo
profufe as fuddenly to endanger life; her
feet and legs fhould be plunged into cold water,
and may remain there as long as they are
fenfibly affected by the cold ; after which,
they fhould be taken out for a few minutes, and then immerfed again. Clyfters of beef water may alfo be injected
cold, and repeated as occafion requires.

So long as ftrength continues, and the
pulfe remains good, it will not be neceffary to proceed to the delivery with
violence, but wait, at leaft for a time,
that the os uteri may relax and dilate by
the effect of pains ; always remem-
bering that the indication of danger is
rather to be taken from the nature of the
fymptoms than the quantity of blood ; as
it is incredible how much fome have loft
and yet furvived ; whilft others will fink
under

under a very inconfiderable difcharge. *Mauriceau* remarks, that where the orifice of the womb was foft, thin, and equal, the patient generally recovered ; but if the contrary, fhe often died ; *Peu*, in his practice of midwifery, feems to be of the fame opinion, and is fo fenfible of the great danger of applying violent force to dilate the os uteri, that he pronounces it death to the patient, from his own experience*.

Delicate women, w ho have lax fibres, of all others, fuftain lofs of blood with moft danger, being extremely apt to faint, and are fubject to violent head-ach. In fuch habits, efpecially after delivery, and in cafes of extreme weaknefs, *hartf- horn jellies*, with rhenifh wine, and thofe things which give nourifhment to the body, and confiftence to the blood, may be advantageoufly directed : A ftrong infu- fion

Peu, Pratique des Accouch. chap. xv. p. 586.

fion of the *cortex* with cinnamon, in French claret, will alfo make a very grateful and generous cordial, without heating the body.

In long-continued fainting-fits, where there was danger of a total ftagnation of blood, I have fometimes directed the following volatile liniment with advantage, to be rubbed upon the pit of the ftomach, in quantity of a tea fpoonful ; over which, a hot flannel fhould afterwards be immediately applied.

R.

Ol. amygd. ℥ *ifs*

Spt. volat. aromat. ℥ *iij mifce & fiat linimentum.*

The fymptoms of immediate danger are principally thefe ; viz. the eyes grow dim, and the extremities cold ; the pulfe becomes weak and intermitting, and the patient frequently faints ; cold fweats, with fubfultus tendinum, or convulfions

fucceed

fucceed, and the hiccough is generally the laft fatal fymptom, which fhews that death is near.

But notwithftanding fome of thofe alarmimg figns, for they feldom all appear, as delivery is the only remedy which can give the patient a chance for life; no one who is truly fenfible of the duties of his profeffion, will timoroufly defert her in the time of her utmoft need, but deliberately follow the rules of practice, and fpeedily endeavour to perform that by *Art*, which *Nature* is unable to accomplifh; without regard to the prejudices of the ignorant vulgar, or that undeferved cenfure which fo frequently follows, where the event is fatal.

Whenever fpeedy delivery becomes abfolutely neceffary, it fhould be attempted without delay, even during the *fainting fits*; for although fuch proceeding may feem to carry with it the appearance of cruelty;

cruelty ; the general relaxation of body which then prevails, will render the uterus more torpid and inactive, and lefs liable to be ftimulated into motion by the hand of the operator ; confequently, as there will be more fpace for turning the child, both it and the mother will fuffer proportionably lefs : Indeed, her lofs of ftrength will concur in making his affiftance more effectual ; the uterus being then, as it were, unbraced and void of contraction : This fhews the folly and imprudence of thofe, who are ever teafing and perfecuting the poor, languifhing, and half-dead patient, with their impertinent admonitions ; " to bear down ftrongly, and make the beft of her labor pains."

In fhort, in all floodings which happen where the *fœtus ftill remains in utero* ; when every other method has failed, and the danger is great ; the patient, if poffible, fhould be *fpeedily delivered* ; and whenever

a

a profuſe hæmorrhage happens *after delivery*, and obſtinately continues notwithſtanding the uſe of the remedies already mentioned ; it will then become neceſſary to throw up *ſtyptic injections* into the uterus, as the laſt and moſt powerful application that can be tried for her relief.

I have been more particular on this my *New Method of treating Uterine Hæmorrhages* by the action of *cold* externally and internally applied to the human body, being convinced, by *repeated experience*, that from thence, the lives of many women may be ſaved, who would be loſt by being treated in the uſual manner.

I did propoſe to make ſome experiments, in order to aſcertain the different quantities of blood eſcaping from the veſſels of wounded animals, expoſed to different degrees of *heat* and *cold* ; but want of opportunity, as well as the cruelty attending ſuch enquiries, have hitherto prevented me.

Beſides

Befides the hæmorrhages incident to pregnant women, there are two other forts which occur more rarely, and not attended with fo much immediate danger; the firft may happen to *virgins*, the laft to women about the difappearance of the menfes.

According to *Lamotte*, thofe floodings to which young women are fubject, arife chiefly from *plethora*, and if the uterus is in a found ftate, are generally remedied by bleeding, laxatives, and abftemious diet. In fuch cafes, we fhould be cautious not to injure the patient's reputation from the fuggeftion that fhe is with child, and that fuch a flux of blood denotes mifcarriage, which fometimes has inadvertently been done.

The menftrul flux, which now and then continues in plethoric habits, for the firft three or four months of pregnancy, and alfo that difcharge of blood which naturally happens after delivery, from the feparation

Y   of

of the placenta, fhould be carefully diftinguifhed from a real flooding, by thofe who
are unexperienced, or who from want of attention rather than judgment, might chance
to fall into miftakes of this kind.

Women about the age of forty-five or
fifty, are fometimes fubject to a difcharge of grumous, fœtid blood, efpecially
thofe of plethoric habits, who are fedentary,
and indulge themfelves to excefs in eating
and drinking.

Dr. *Amb. Dawfon*, formerly an eminent
phyfician of extenfive practice in London,
affures me, that he has often given *cremor.
tart.* in fuch hæmorrhages with remarkable
fuccefs.

When the female conftitution continues
to generate redundant blood beyond the
ftated time of nature, and where the uterine veffels, from the effect of age, become
rigid and compact too early, fo as to prevent its paffing off that way, great inconve-
niences to health are the confequences of
it,

it, though in general, they may either be relieved or cured by bleeding and evacuations:
However, when such complaints are of long
continuance, attended with flow fever, a sanious difcharge, and painful forcing down
of the affected part, they almoft certainly
denote a difeafed uterus, and frequently
prove mortal in the conclufion.

As for the *extract. cicutæ*, its effects in
fuch cafes have by no means equalled my
expectation, confidering the extravagant encomiums with which it was ufhered into
practice. The *vegeto-mineral water* recommended by *Goulard*, may be tried as an injection; and *opiates*, after gentle evacuations,
where the pain is violent, may be directed
to advantage. I have obferved very fenfible, and good effects from the ufe of *Peruvian bark* in the following form, though a
perfect cure is not always to be expected.

℞

> *Cort. Peruv. fubtilifs. Pulv.* ℥ i
> *Cremor Tart.* ʒ iii
> *Pulp. Tamarind.* ℥ fs

Syr.

Syr. caryoph. rub. q. s. ut fiat elect. cujus sumat. quant. nucis moschat. nocteq. Mane.

Vegetable diet, with nourishment of easy digestion, and moderate exercise in pure air, with the chalybeate waters of *Tunbridge* or *Spa*, will likewise promote the cure; or at least will tend to abate the severity of the symptoms, and prolong the patient's life.

SECTION.

SECTION VI.

*Of Convulfions, and Acute Difeafes in general,
moft fatal to Women during the State of Pregnancy.*

THE caufe of convulfions is often feated
in the *brain,* or fuch parts a have immediate intercourfe with it, by mediation of the nerves, particularly the *ftomach*
and *uterus.* They may alfo arife from violent affections of mind, and likewife from
plethora, or *inanition.* There are other more
remote caufes of this difeafe, viz. the fup-
preffion of fome long-accuftomed difcharge,
as eruptions repelled from the bodily
furface; the ftoppage of bleeding piles; or
application of any painful ftimulus to the
nervous parts.

Convulfions are either *idiopathic* or *fymptomatic;* the firft are owing to fome morbid
impreffion originally made on the *brain* or

Y 3

genus

genus nervofum, and when derived from the parent, are termed *hereditary* : The laft arife from accidental caufes which act fuddenly on the nerves, and with more violence than their natural ftructure can bear. Thofe which are hereditary or habitual, and which continue after puberty, are generally incurable, though feldom mortal ; and when they totally difappear about that period ; it feems owing to a gradual change produced in the body, by the effect of age, which leffens its *irritability*, and gives more ftrength and firmnefs to the whole folid fyftem.

A remarkable alteration is likewife brought about in the female habit, towards the firft eruption of menfes ; for at this time, convulfions have been known to ceafe, which before had refifted the moft efficacious remedies.

Hyfterical women, from delicacy of habit, and the great irritability of their nerves, are, of all others, the moft fubject

to

to this malady, especially during the latter end of their *first pregnancy*. This probably arises from the uncommon pressure of the gravid uterus on the abdominal viscera, which may obstruct their vessels, and prevent the free circulation of blood ; or else from the vast distension of uterine fibres, which creates pain, and by nervous sympathy, throws the whole vascular system into a convulsive spasm. But that this violent and unaccustomed stress laid on the uterus, by the increased bulk of the child, is not alone sufficient to produce the disease is evident ; seeing, that gravid women in general are not subject to it ; and therefore, the *original cause* must have pre-existed in the constitution either from some former injury done to the *brain*, or a morbid impression derived from the parent, which remains dormant and inactive, until excited into motion by such change as that arising from pregnancy.

Y 4

A.

As the caufes of convulfions are various, fo likewife is the intention of cure. The veffels of the body can neither be filled or emptied beyond a certain degree, without occafioning *plethora* in one cafe, and *inanition* in the other, both which extremes are deftructive to health, and may occafion convulfions. In the firft, they arife from painful diftenfion of the nervous parts; and in the laft, from a defect of the circulating power, and that equal diftribution of blood, which is neceffary to carry on the feveral fecretions.

Convulfions from *inanition*, are much more dangerous than thofe from *plethora*; as it is eafier to empty than replenifh the veffels; for, although nourifhment may be taken into the ftomach; it is a confiderable time before it can be converted into blood, efpecially where the affimilating powers of the body have been much impaired.

When this difeafe comes on after profufe floodings, or other immoderate evacuations, it it is *generally mortal* ; and it may be obferved that flaughtered animals, having loft a certain quantity of blood, fall into convulfions a fhort time before death. *Van Swieten* fuppofes, that this is owing to the uniform preffure of the blood veffels being fuddenly taken off from the *brain* ; but more probably, it happens becaufe that equilibrium or balance is deftroyed, which ought to fubfift between the folids and fluids ; and therefore as foon as the quantity and impulfe of blood on its containing veffels become deficient ; the vafcular fyftem, for want of due refiftance, begins to exert a kind of preternatural contractive power, and the whole bodily frame is agitated or convulfed.

But notwithftanding what has been faid ; the above author relates the following extraordinary cafe, where the patient recovered.*
Novi gravidam, quæ placidiffime dormiverat, dum in vicinia periculofum erat incendium : Sollicita mater, mane accurrens, gratulabatur filiæ, quod blandus fomnus omnem timorem arcuiffet.
Mox

---

* *Van Swieten*, Comment. Vol. iv. p. 497.

Mox incipit tremere mifera toto corpore, & angi, fimulque totus lectus jam inundabatur fanguine, fequente animi deliquio, & convulfionibus ; tamen a periculofa hac Uteri Hæmorrhagia convaluit, fed fœtum quadrimeftrem abortiens perdidit.

Medicines, in fuch cafes, are in a manner out of the queftion ; for nothing will fo effectually reftore ftrength, as the repeated ufe of nourifhing fluids, in fmall quantities : Broth clyfters may alfo be adminiftered ; and if the pulfe fhould remain very weak and languid ; a decoction of *Peruvian bark* may be given, with warm nervous cordials, joined with an *opiate*, fuch as the *confect. paulin. &c.* Where the fymptoms are urgent, and the circulation almoft at a ftand ; *blifters* may be applied to infide of the arms, and finapifms to the foles of the feet ; the extremities may alfo be rubbed with hot flannels, or immerfed in *warm water*, the effect of which, has already been confidered.

When

When convulfions arife from *plethora*, which chiefly happens to fuch as are young, who indulge their appetite, and have a ftrong digeftion ; the pulfe is generally hard, full, and frequent, which will require the immediate and repeated lofs of blood, with the ufe of laxative medicines and plentiful dilution. The *faline draughts* with *nitre* may be given, and the patient fhould be enjoined to ufe light and abftemious diet, for fear of a relapfe.

When fhe is comatofe during the intervals, and her head affected, the eyes being prominent and blood-fhot, attended with delirium, or much fever ; the ufe of *opiates* are improper: In fhort, they ought not to be given, except in cafes of great urgency from pain or want of fleep, and even then, only after bleeding and evacuations.

It is of the utmoft confequence to diftinguifh the true caufe of convulfions, before any medicines are prefcribed, or methods tried for the patient's relief ; as an error of judgment

judgment might here prove of fatal confequence : For inftance, · copious bleeding which would relieve or cure convulfions arifing from *plenitude,* would inftantly deftroy the patient, if they were brought on by *inanition* ; and *emetics,* which would be proper when the ftomach was loaded with bile or other noxious humors, would be highly pernicious, where they were occafioned by ardent fever, or *inflammation of the brain.*

Thofe of ftrong, robuft conftitutions, are feldom fubject to convulfions, except from violent caufes ; on the contrary, children, and women of delicate habits, are fometimes affected by the flighteft impreffions on the body or mind ; and it is remarkable, that what produces very extraordinary and alarming fymptoms in one, will not at all endanger another ; each feeling the effects of different caufes, according to their natural temperament, and as their nerves are ftrung to different fenfations. But although women and children are more fubject to this

disease

difeafe than men, in proportion as their habit is weak and irritable, it is obferved that they efcape the danger of it much better.

Convulfions fupervening violent fevers, or inflammation of the brain, are aften mortal ; but thofe which are followed by fever, critical eruptions on the body, or a difcharge of putrid bile from the ftomach or inteftines, generally end more favorably. If they are of the hyfterical kind, unattended by *coma, delirium* or *fever,* and attack the patient, by long intervals, fo as to become habitual, they do not denote immediate danger ; but fometimes occafion palfy, lofs of memory, or idiotifm, by gradually impairing the vital functions.

When this difeafe is fuddenly produced by *terror* ; *bleeding,* the liberal ufe of *opiates,* and *warm bath,* by diffolving the fpafm and foothing the nerves, will beft anfwer the intention of cure.

I

I attended a lady in the year 1776, who was repeatedly attacked with convulsions during pregnancy, which were first owing to a fright, and to which she had been subject many years; being treated in the manner just mentioned, she went on the full time of her pregnancy, and being happily delivered, recovered without any relapse.

Some authors recommend bleeding *in* the foot, when the head is affected; but the doctrine of *derivation* and *revulsion*, as applied to bleeding, is not less inconsistent and irrational, than in what it relates to the *pediluvium* or warm bath for the feet. Opening a vein in the foot, has been said to bring on the menses; when blood drawn from the arm, had no such effect; and this was supposed to happen in consequence of its accelerating the blood's motion through the vessels of the legs and *uterus*, which indeed is a downright contradiction; for when a vein is opened in any part, the motion of blood through it, *pro tempore*, will

rather

rather be retarded than increafed ; as it is evident that the *bleeding orifice* cannot poffibly tranfmit fo much blood as the trunk of the vein, before its compreffion by the ligature.   Admitting this as a fact, it will follow, that if menfes have been fuddenly brought on by bleeding in the foot, the effect was produced in a manner directly contrary to what has generally been imagined, viz. from compreffion of the veins and arteries by the *ligature* applied, and to *immerfion* of the feet in hot water, both which, as already remarked, increafe the quantity and velocity of blood paffing through the *uterus*.

Errors in diet, or food taken into the ftomach which offends in quantity and quality, have been known to occafion convulfions ; but thefe are feldom dangerous, and generally ceafe, as foon as the offending

matter

* Page 258, et feq.

matter is evacuated, by giving an *emetic* and laxatives; after which an opiate will be proper.

Retention of Urine, by diftending the bladder and creating violent pain, may likewife be productive of convulfions, efpecially in weak, irritable habits ; but here, as in the former cafe, they foon go off, after it has been emptied by the *catheter ;* otherwife, a warm bath fhould be directed, with emulfions and anodyne clyfters.

When the neck of the urinary bladder is compreffed by the child's head, it may be gently raifed above the fymphyfis of the pubes : A cafe of this kind, is mentioned in *Lamotte*'s obfervations, where, from fuch affiftance only, a large quantity of urine was inftantly difcharged.

A patient at the *Weftminfter Lying-In Hofpital,* about two years ago, in the time of labor, complained of exceffive pain at the pubes, which fhe was not able to endure

without

without crying aloud : She was feized with fubfultus tendinum, which occafioned the Matron to fend for me : I found the bladder diftended with water, and raifed above the brim of the pelvis, fo that during her labor pains it was violently compreffed between the uterus and bones, even to the danger of burfting ; I directed the water immediately to be drawn off by the *catheter*, after which fhe became eafy, and was delivered foon after.

Another cafe of the like kind happened at the *Hofpital* lately ; where the bladder, by its hardnefs and projection over the pubes in the time of labor, was at firft miftaken for the child's head : This patient was treated in the fame manner as the former, and alfo recovered.

Where *cutaneous eruptions* are fuddenly thrown back into the habit ; the *warm bath*, and gentle *diaphoretics* with nitre, will bid fair to relieve the patient : but fhould her complaints arife from *worms* ; anthelmin-

Z   tic

tic medicines may be given, in which, *Plenck's* preparation of mercury, with gum arabic, is both efficacious and safe, if administered with due caution. The *Indian Pink Root* ; the bark of the wild cabbage or *bulge water tree* of Jamaica ; and the *coubage*, the pods of which are lined with the *siliqua hirsuta* of *Linnæus*, have all lately been recommended as powerful medicines for this purpose ; but I cannot say much of them from my own experience, except the *Indian Pink Root*, an infusion of which, is both elegant and efficacious.

In strong *convulsions* during pregnancy, speedy delivery has been proposed, and recurred to as the principal remedy : but observation and experience shew, that this rule will admit of many exceptions, and ought to be regarded with great caution ; especially by those who are young in practice, and therefore influenced by fear, which naturally suggests the worst ; in consequence of which, they are often prompted

to

to proceed with more haste and violence than is confiftent with the patient's fafety.

It has already been remarked, that fimple preffure of the *gravid uterus* on the contiguous vifcera may interrupt the natural functions of thofe parts, and occafion convulfions; and to fuch cafes, may be added thofe where that part is defective in its organical ftructure; and being either too fmall, or preternaturally firm and compact, cannot yield fufficiently to the increafed bulk of the child, without being violently diftended and overftrained; or elfe by an unfavorable pofition of the fœtus, it may be compreffed and bruifed between the angular parts of its body and bones of the pelvis, fo as to excite pain, and bring on convulfions; efpecially, as the habit is at this time uncommonly irritable. Under fuch circumftances fpeedy delivery, if the patient is at, or near her full time, may procure her inftant relief; but on the contrary, whenever they arife from any caufe

Z 2 *independent*

independent of the state of pregnancy; experience, as well as reason, evidently shew, that delivery thus violently brought about, contrary to the common course of nature, would not only prove ineffectual, but highly dangerous.

Hoffman supposes that the *duodenum* is often the seat of convulsions, because of the discharge of bile and pancreatic juice, into the cavity of that intestine ; which from various causes are wont to become putrid and highly acrimonious ; consequently, they may produce great pain and tumult in the body, if not soon evacuated by gentle cathartics.

The retention of these *acrimonious salts* and *rancid oils* which naturally ought to pass off by the kidnies, may likewise occasion this malady ; as it has sometimes been observed to succeed a flux of pale, limpid urine, especially in fevers : In such cases, small portions of *emetic tartar*, with the saline draughts,. or other saponaceous fluids have been found to procure relief.

Besides

. Befides the feveral caufes of convulfive diforders already enumerated, there may be others, fo latent and difficult to be found out, as to remain imperceptible to the niceft obferver ; which neverthelefs act with great violence on the fenfible and irritable parts of human bodies. In fuch doubtful cafes, or where the patient is fenfelefs and can give no information ; the indication of cure muft be taken from the general methods of treating the difeafe, and the precipitate adminiftration of powerful medicines ought to be avoided ; for he that is afraid of miftaking his way, fhould rather abate than redouble his fpeed. If the patient is unable to fwallow, which frequently happens, fhe fhould nct be neglected on that account ; fince *opium*, *mufk*, or other medicines may be advantageoufly given in clyfters.

Women who have been fubject to the difeafe, in former pregnancy, fhould ufe every poffible caution to avoid it ; by

Z 3

bleeding,

bleeding, the use of *opiates*, or such other medicines or methods, as seem best appropriated to the nature of their conftitution, before the approach of labor.

The violence, and long duration of convulfions, fometimes leave a *morbid impreffion* on the brain or nerves, by which the intellectual faculties are much impaired. In fuch cafes, blifters, preparations of *bark*, with aromatic bitters, or the warm foetid gums, have been found ferviceable ; alfo chalybeate waters ; the cold bath, and moderate exercife, in a dry, pure air.

℞

  Pulv. fubtilliff. Cort. Peruv. ℥ *i*
  ――*radic. Valerian. Sylv.* ℥ *iij*
  Chalyb. rubig. preparat.
  Spec. Aromat. aa ℥ *i*
 Syr. Caryoph. rub. q. f. ut fiat Elect. cujus fumat quant. Nucis mofchat. bis terve in die, fuperbibend. Cyath. Aq. Pyrmont. vel Spadan.

        All

All animal and vegetable fubftances, which are ufually directed in fpafmodic complaints, act by their powerful effluvia, and in a certain degree feem to produce a narcotic effect ; among the firft are mufk, and caftor ; and of the laft are gum affafœtid. fagap. camphor, valerian, &c. but *opium*, where-ever it can be properly given, is the fovereign medicine, and fuperior to all the reft.

Here it is neceffary to caution young prac-titioners, who are generally *enthufiafts* in phy-fic, not to imagine that the names of medi-cines, or the clafs to which they belong, either fufficiently denote their true qualities or point out their real ufe : They ought not therefore, to depend upon them too much, however dignified with the appel-lation of *antifpafmodics*, *fpecifics*, &c. many of them have not even power enough to do harm ; which indeed is faying fomething in their favor ; fince thofe which are good, are often abufed, and then become the worft of all.   Z 4   The

The means of making remedies falutary, confift in diftinguifhing properly how they are to be applied : Thus adminiftered, there is much which they will do, but much more which it is impoffible they fhould do, from the very nature of things ; and which therefore, it would be unphilofophical as well as unreafonable to expect.

I was favored with the following cafe by Mr. *M——n*, the gentleman who attended and delivered the patient ; and have fet it down, as near as poffible, in his own words.

C A S E I.

Mrs. *D——an*, of *Swallow-ftreet*, aged thirty, at her full time, and with her firft child, was feized on the 24th of *January*, 1764, with violent and univerfal convulfions, in the beginning of labor, whilft her pains were moderate, attended

with

with total deprivation of her senses : Being
of a plethoric habit, twelve or fourteen
ounces of blood were immediately taken
from the arm ; a blister was applied to the
back, and the usual antispasmodic medicines administered, but without any sensible benefit ; the convulsions increased in
frequency and violence ; recurring every
five or six minutes, without any intervals of
respite : At the accession of every fit, the
child's head was pressed down on the *os uteri*,
as if a labor pain had been coming on ;
it then grew rigid, and the agitation of the
whole body was so violent, that there was
no possibility of obtaining any farther information from the touch : In the mean time
the arm, from struggling, bled to the quantity of ten or twelve ounces more, but no
faintings ensued. In this manner, when
about eight hours had elapsed, and no
symptoms of amendment appeared ; it was
proposed to bring the child away by instru-
ments, and for the satisfaction of her friends

and

and the preservation of the attendant's character, to request Dr. *Leake's* advice; and that he would be present during the operation; but as his residence was distant, and the first messenger had mistaken the street, upwards of an hour was lost, before he was apprised of it; and in the mean time, the *convulsions* increased to such a degree, that her death was every moment expected. In the intervals, which were now very short, no pulse was to be felt, nor could she be perceived to breathe: Her attendant therefore thinking that farther delay might be fatal, resolved not to wait any longer, but proceed to the operation. During the recess of the convulsions, he could perceive the os uteri was dilated to a considerable extent, and the head advanced below the brim of the pelvis: After repeated trials with the *short forceps*, finding he could not succeed, on account of the height and largeness of the head, and the insufficient dilation of the os uteri; he

introduced

introduced the *fciffars*, perforated the fcull, and after evacuating its contents, extracted the bones of the head ; and then delivered her without much difficulty. Juſt as the operation was finiſhed, Dr. *Leake* arrived, and feeing the ftate of the patient, confirmed the unfavorable prognoftic which her attendant had before made : However, thinking it better to try the effect of doubtful remedies than none, he prefcribed for her as follows.

R.
    Pulv. e Myrrh. c. Əj
    Mofch,
    Sal. Succin. ạa Ə ſſ
    Syr. e Cort. Aurant. q. ſ. ut fiat Bolus ạta quaq. hora ſumend. cum Cyath. Julep. ſequent.

R.
    Julep. e Camphor, ℥ *viij*
    Spt. Volat. fœtid. ℥ *ij mifce.*

Sinapiſms were alfo directed to be applied to the foles of the feet.

On

On the third day from her delivery, she began gradually to return to her senses, as if waking out of a dream ; but had not the least recollection of any thing that had happened, or of any pain she felt since the time her *Accoucheur* first entered the room. In a fortnight she perfectly recovered, and since that time has had several children.

C A S E   II.

August the 6th, 1765, I was sent for to see a gentlewoman at *Camberwell*, who was convulsed ; she was big with the first child, and at the full expiration of her reckoning; her midwife was with her, and informed me she had no labor-pains, the *os uteri* not being at all dilated. She was apparently of a strong habit of body, and had been remarkably healthy during the latter end of pregnancy : The fits, two in number. which had been violent, were gone off before I saw her : Her pulse was good, and she was perfectly sensible, but could give no man-

ner

ner of reason for her complaint: I ordered twelve ounces of blood to be drawn, and a cathartic clyster to be administered ; after which, she took a bolus, with *musk* and *opium*, and washed it down with the saline mixture. When I saw her next day, in the afternoon, she seemed in a manner quite recovered ; but had only taken her medicines once. She was delivered two days after, and did well.

C A S E III.

October the 28th, 1769, late at night, I was desired to visit Mrs. *A—d—n,* in *Cavendish-Square,* who was suddenly attacked with convulsions, the third day after delivery, without any apparent cause : She was naturally of a very chearful, volatile disposition, but subject to a *nervous tremor* on the slightest occasion. The convulsive spasms were gone off before I got there ; but her voice was tremulous and indistinct, her eyes wild and staring, and her intellect very imperfect ;

perfect; she swallowed with great difficulty, and her face was much altered from its
former appearance : Her pulse was frequent,
weak, and unequal ; sometimes vibrating
with uncommon velocity, and then suddenly intermitting, and becoming almost imperceptible, for the space of one or two pul-
sations. Her friends did not know she had
been disturbed, nor could I find by the nurse,
that any thing had been given to eat or
drink which disagreed with her ; but as I
had attended her before, and found that
opiates generally relieved her, I prescribed
the following medicines.

℞

    Pil. e Styrace gr. vj
    Pulv. Castor. r. ℈ß
  *Balsam. Peruv. q. f. ut fiat bolus minim. pro
re nata exhibend. cum cochlear. duobus Julepi
sequentis.*

℞.   *Julep. e Camphor. ℥ v*
    Aq. Puleg simp. ℥ iij
    Spt. Volat. foetid. ℥ ij fiat Julepum.

                        Before

Before seven in the evening, she had taken two boluses, and having had some refreshing sleep, waked sensible and seemed better; when I saw her at that time, her pulse was more full and strong; and as there appeared no signs of relapse, the application of a blister was omitted, to which she seemed much averse: I desired that three spoonful of the *Julep* might now be given occasionally, without the bolus; except she was threatened with convulsions.

Next morning she was still better, having passed a good night: In the evening she complained of pain at her stomach, but was free from feverish symptoms, and perspired gently. The *emplast. stomachic.* was directed to the pit of her stomach; her feet were wrapped in hot flannels, and the use of the julep was omitted. She now continued recovering every day, but towards the end of the month, being subject to night sweats; she took a decoction of the *cortex*, with *elix. vitriol. dulc.* which restored her to perfect health. CASE

C A S E IV.

Sarah Silby, of a strong athletic habit, was delivered in the *Westminster Lying-In Hospital* the 26th of August, 1771. The labor was natural, and the placenta came away with ease about an hour after delivery, as I was informed by the gentleman who at that time attended the hospital; she appeared well as could be expected till nine in the evening, when she complained of great sickness and oppression at her stomach, and vomitted a large quantity of *poraceous bile:* As the sickness did not entirely go off, a grain of *emetic tartar* was directed to cleanse her stomach more thoroughly; but it did not produce any sensible effect. About midnight, she was attacked with violent *convulsions*, which lasted till eleven o'clock the next day; during which time she had ten or eleven fits, and twice or thrice threw up phlegm, mixed with clots of blood; but as she was senseless and

the

comatofe in the intervals, it was not poffible to adminifter any kind of medicine.

The 27th in the morning, her pulfe was hard and oppreffed, her fkin hot and dry, and overfpread with a deep yellow, as if fhe had been ill with the *jaundice*. The tongue was foul, and had been wounded by her teeth in the convulfive paroxyfms; fo that it appeared, the blood which fhe had difcharged, did not proceed from her ftomach, but only from her mouth: The abdomen was tenfe and fwelled, and fhe breathed with much difficulty. Ten ounces of blood were immediately taken from the arm, and a *cathartic clyfter* was afterwards adminiftered. In the evening fhe was better; the clyfter had procured her three ftools, and leffened the hardnefs and fwelling of her belly.

I then directed one of the following powders, to be taken every four hours, and an anodyne draught to be given the laft thing at night. A a ℞. *Tart.*

℞.

  Tart. emet. gr. iſs

Magnes. alb. ℥ *iſs contere & f. pulv. in ſex portiones dividendus.*

℞.

  Aq. Puleg. ℥ *iſs*

  Spt. Volat. fœtid. ℥ *ij*

  Tinct. Thebaic. gu xxx

  Syr. e Cort. Aurant. ℥ *j miſce & fiat hauſtus.*

The 28th in the morning, ſhe was ſenſible and much relieved, her pulſe was more ſoft and equal ; the powders had brought on a free perſpiration, and the ſuffuſſion of bile on her ſkin was leſs perceptible ; The opiate had alſo procured her ſome refreſhing ſleep, but as I obſerved her head was diſordered, and affected with *ſtupor, leeches* were directed to be applied to her temples in the evening.

29th. Better in all reſpects, and perfectly fenſible, but complained of the foreneſs of her tongue, which was waſhed with ſage-tea and honey : In the evening, ſhe was feveriſh, and

and had muscular pains in different parts of her body, but remained perfectly sensible. The antimonial powders were continued.

30th. The preceding night's rest, and a free perspiration, had remedied her yesterday's complaints : Nothing was now given but nourishing food of easy digestion, by which, her strength sensibly increased, and in a few days she perfectly recovered.

CASE V.

That part of the following case, which relates to the different circumstances of labor, I took from the minutes of one of my *Pupils*, who then attended in rotation and delivered the patient ; the rest is set down according to the best of my recollection.

Ann Philips, on *Thursday* morning, the 27th of *February*, 1772, about two o'clock, was brought into the *Hospital*, with symptoms of approaching labor ; the waters

A a 2   were

were discharged the preceding evening, but her pains were inconsiderable ; at last they became stronger, and returing by shorter intervals, brought the head below the brim of the pelvis, which was narrow ; about three o'clock in the afternoon, her pains were still more frequent, but of shorter duration ; notwithstanding, the head made some small advances, and continued to do so until about eight o'clock, when it was totally disengaged from the uterus, and the birth was expected at every pain. Her pulse was now strong, full and frequent, as it had continued during the day ; when, after changing the situation of her body, which was unfavorable, she seemed rather fatigued, and was suddenly seized with *convulsive spasms* in both legs, which quickly increased, and soon affected her whole body ; Her pulse, during the fit, was small and very quick ; she had seemingly great anxiety and oppression about the *praecordia*, and the urine was discharged infensibly ; The spasm continued

continued about ten minutes, when she was
apparently quite recovered ; her pulse also
grew stronger, but her pains were manifestly interrupted, and much weaker. The
convulsions returned by intervals of near
an hour, and were of long duration,
'till about twelve o'clock, when she was
delivered. She was afterwards much better,
but her fits again returned in half an hour
with greater violence than ever ; her intellect, during the intervals, being also very
imperfect.

Eight ounces of blood were taken away,
and the following bolus directed to be given
immediately after, and repeated as occasion
should require :

℞.

 Extract. Thebaic. gr. iss
 Mosch. Əss
 Confect. Alkerm. q. s. ut fiat bolus

She was strongly convulsed in the night
several times, and by seven o'clock in the
morning, had thirteen fits from the first

A a 3

attack

attack ; about nine she was better, but complained of much pain in her head, and soreness all over her body.

An emollient clyster was administered, and her temples were bathed with warm vinegar, the fumes of which, she also drew up her nose : Her head being affected, the *opiate* was omitted, but about nine at night, it was repeated, left there should be a return of the convulsions. The next morning she was much better in all respects ; had found, refreshing sleep in the night, and perspired freely. From this time the symptoms of weakness gradually went off, and in a few days she perfectly recovered.

C A S E   VI.

I was favoured with the particulars of the following case, by Mr. *H——t*, an *apothecary* in town, who practises midwifery, and at whose request I was sent for, at the time the patient was seized with convulsions.

Mrs.

Mrs. *H——*, the wife of a tradefman in *James-ftreet, Covent Garden* ; about thirty years of age, of a robuft, plethoric habit, and perfectly healthy ; being pregnant with her firft child, was feized with *convulfions* at the expiration of her full time, and during labor, *viz.* the 10th of *March*, 1772 : Her pulfe was full, and her pains feemed natural, but fo moderate, that fhe was not at firft examined by the touch : In lefs than an hour, fhe was taken with retching without any apparent caufe, and complained of pain at her ftomach : A little warm caudle was given her, which was inftantly thrown up ; the pain at her ftomach became violent and the vomitting increafed ; about half an hour after, fhe was feized with *ftrong convulfions*, which ceafed by intervals ; fhe vomitted with great violence, and feveral times threw up a large quantity of flimy fluid, mixed with blood.

During this time, there were no figns of labor, the *os uteri* being rigid and quite closed.

A a 4

closed : Every paroxysm was succeeded by a seeming profound sleep, attended with snoring, or rather snorting, with a discharge of foam from her mouth, mixed with blood. She was in this situation when I first saw her. Twelve ounces of blood were immediately taken away, a *blistering plaster* was applied to the nape of her neck, and *sinapisms* to the soles of her feet : I prescribed a bolus with *musk* and *opium*, which being dissolved, was swallowed with some difficulty. She continued speechless and insensible, as she had been from the first attack, but the convulsions left her, and the labor pains grew stronger ; the *os uteri* then dilated, and the child advanced at every pain, insomuch that the birth was speedily expected : On a sudden, the pulse sunk, and her strength being perceived to lessen every moment ; the child which was dead, was extracted by the *forceps*, and in about three hours after she expired.

I

I could not perceive that the tongue was wounded, as it frequently is in such cafes; and therefore fuppofed that the blood difcharged from her mouth, proceeded from a ruptured veffel in the ftomach; otherwife an *emetic* would have been proper, fince the vaft quantity of glairy, *gaftric fluid* thrown up, denoted fomething amifs in that part; which, like the urinary bladder, when irritated by a ftone, or the inteftines, when any painful ftimulus is applied, feparate the fame kind of mucus in great abundance.

CASE VII.

Auguft the 12th, 1772, at feven o'clock in the morning, I was defired, as foon as poffible, to vifit a gentlewoman at *Lambeth*, who was feized with convulfions, and fuppofed to be in labor. Her firft midwife feeing the ftate fhe was in, and fearing, I fuppofe, fhe would die, pretended bufinefs elfewhere, and left her. The midwife who

who was afterwards sent for, being present, informed me her pains were inconsiderable, and that the *os uteri* was very little dilated. Her nails were black, and her arms had repeatedly been drawn up with great violence towards her body, as if affected with the *cramp*. She complained of intolerable pain in her bowels, and was much oppressed with wind at her stomach, which was tense and swelled; her pulse was frequent and irregular: and I was told she had long labored under great anxiety of mind and dejection of spirits, as well as bodily pain. Her extremities were ordered to be gently rubbed with warm cloths, and afterwards to be wrapped in hot flannels. I directed the following draught, and also an emollient clyster to be administered:

℞

> *Confect. cardiac.* ℥ss
> *Aq. Menth. pip. simp.* ℥iss
> *Nucis Moschat.* ℨiij
> *Tinct. Thebaic.* g¹¹. xx

Syr.

Syr. e Mecon. ʒj fiat hauſtus anodyn.
quamprimum exhibendus.

As ſhe continued in great pain, and ſome
ſymptoms of *convulſive ſpaſms* appearing in
the evening; ſeven ounces of blood were
taken away, and the anodyne draught was
repeated : She diſcharged large quantities of
wind from her ſtomach, and was ſo much
relieved from pain, that ſhe fell into a profound ſleep, and was much better in all reſpects the next morning; after which her
labor pains came on, and being happily delivered about one o'clock the ſame day, ſhe
ſoon perfectly recovered.

Dr. *Gaubius,* in his *Adverſaria,* mentions
the internal uſe of the flowers of *zinc,* and
informs us that he directed them with ſuc-
ceſs in the cure of *convulſive and ſpaſmodic
diſeaſes*; but ſuch is the almoſt infinite variety of cauſes from whence convulſions
may proceed, that what will relieve or totally remove them in one, will not be found
in the leaſt beneficial to another; and I
think

think it still remains for further experience to determine, whether their medicinal effects in such cases, are to be depended upon or not. Six grains of the flowers of *zinc* may be mixed with a dram of fine sugar, and being divided into six parts, one of them may be given thrice a-day, or oftener, as occasion requires.

NEXT to Uterine Hæmorrhages and Convulsions ; the *Pleurisy*, *Dysentery* and *Small-Pox*, deserve attention, as diseases of a very destructive nature to women during pregnancy : But as they have been fully and judiciously considered by authors of the greatest eminence ; I shall only take a cursory view of them, in order to shew how much their dangerous tendency is then increased ; as well as to point out that peculiarity of treatment, which they at this time require.

As

As a firm and compact ſtate of the ſolids are obſerved to produce *acute diſeaſes*; ſo lax fibres and a delicate habit diſpoſe the body to thoſe of the *chronic kind.* Women, there-fore, are found to be much leſs ſubject to *pleuriſy* than men; and thoſe who have a bad digeſtion and phlegmatic conſtitution, are ſeldom affected with it at all; according to that aphoriſm of *Hippocrates* : *Qui acidum eructant, raro pleuritici fiunt.*

Although ſtrong maſculine women who uſe hard exerciſe, and where the menſes have been deficient, are much oftener viſited with it than others; I have ſeen two or three inſtances, where thoſe of a very con-trary kind were alſo violently affected*. The production of the diſeaſe, and its ſymp-toms, may therefore, probably ſometimes ariſe from a defect of the *vis vitæ*, as well as from exceſs of it; for inſtance, when the quantity of animal fluids is much leſſened, in valetudinary, exhauſted women, ſo is

their

* Vide *Child-bed Fever*, page 223.

their ftrength likewife ; and confequently, four ounces of blood, which fhall accidently become redundant, will render fuch women as *plethoric*, and over-load their veffels as much at one time, as double the quantity would have done at another, when they were ftronger.

In the beginning of the difeafe, the pulfe is commonly hard, full, and ftrong ; but when the pain in the fides becomes acute and refpiration very difficult, it then lofes its firmnefs, and grows more foft and weak; and as the blood cannot now pafs through the lungs, they will begin to participate of the inflammation ; and the *pleurify* will then be complicated with the *peripneumony*.

Without this diftinction, and particular regard to alteration of the pulfe ; *bleeding* would often be omitted, as improper, even when moft conducive to the patient's fafety, by preventing a *mortal fuffocation* ; for fhe is often cut off by the difficulty of breathing, and the confequent obftruction of blood in the

the lungs, before the inflammation has brought on any collection of *matter* in the thorax. The indication of cure, is therefore, rather to be taken from *respiration*, than the state of the pulse, which manifestly depends upon the former.

Servius who opened a great number of those who died of the *pleurify* at *Rome*, always found one lobe of the lungs corrupted, but the *pleura* was either slightly affected, or altogether untouched by the inflammation.

In most acute fevers of the inflammatory kind; scarcely any thing is required, besides well-timed evacuations, with plentiful dilution ; and therefore, *bleeding, gentle laxatives, and the faline mixture with nitre,* will here be proper ; especially, when the skin is dry, and the pulse hard and full.

When the patient is much relieved in the beginning, by profuse perspiration, and the pulse becomes more soft and free ; or

where

where she is benefited by expectoration in the progress of the disease ; bleeding does not seem neceffary, but it may be advantageoufly directed at all times, whenever a dangerous difficulty of breathing fuddenly comes on : Under thefe circumftances, it is fafe and requifite in women with child as others ; and even more fo, in thofe who are young, and naturally of a plethoric habit of body, and who are not advanced beyond the *fourth month of pregnancy*; for the *embryo* being then fmall, and not requiring the whole quantity of redundant blood ; nature often finds means to carry it off by the *vagina,* left it fhould over-fill the veffels, and injure the confti-tution.

Where expectoration is fuppreffed, and difficulty of breathing comes on ; *Baglivi* recommends the application of blifters to the infide of the legs, and alfo mentions the remarkable good effects of warm, diluting fluids, taken often and in fmall quantities.

For

For this purpose, nothing can be better calculated than the *decoct. pector.* with nitre; and if the steam of warm water is frequently drawn into the lungs with the breath, it will be found beneficial.

Where the pain is extremely acute during respiration; swathing or binding the thorax with a broad circular bandage, will often procure great relief, by preventing the elevation of the sternum, and distension of the affected parts; for then, breathing is principally carried on by a greater depression of the diaphragm, at each inspiration; but this would be highly improper in *gravid women*, where the whole abdominal cavity being taken up by the *inlarged uterus*, the motion of the lungs would, in a manner, be suppressed, and the patient suffocated. *Emetics*, for the same reason, should be omitted, or given with the greatest caution; especially in full habits, before bleeding, or where signs of *delirium* appear.

B b

To

To promote expectoration, either of the following medicines may be directed, according to the degree of inflammation, and nature of the symptoms :

℞.

    Ol. Lini per expre∫s. ℨ *iij*

    Spt. Sal. ammoniac. g^{tt}. xx

    Aq. Puleg. ∫imp. ℥ *i∫s*

    Oxymel. Scillit. ℨ*j fiat hau∫tus* ℥*ta quaq. hora ∫umendus.*

℞.

    Sal. Ab∫inth. Э *i*

    Succ. Limon. ℥ *∫s*

    Sperm. Ceti ∫olut. ℨ *∫s*

    Aq. Hy∫∫op. ℥ *x*

    Syr. bal∫amic ℥ *i fiat hau∫tus.*

The application of a *bli∫tering pla∫ter* to the affected part seems most rational after bleeding, &c. but where-ever the pain is fixed, and so acute, as to occasion much difficulty of breathing in the beginning; it may then be directed with great safety and advantage, as I have observed several times.

times. In short, the treatment of this difeafe in *pregnant women*, with fome exceptions, is nearly the fame as in thofe who are not fo, although the event is much more dangerous; according to *Hippocrates*, viz. *Mulierem in utero gerentem, ab acuto aliquo morbo corripi, lethale.*

Mrs. *M-y-les* of *Weftminfter*, aged thirty-two, and of a weakly conftitution; in the fourth month of her pregnancy, was feized with an *acute, inflammatory fever*, fuppofed to have been communicated by her hufband, who was then recovering from a dangerous illnefs of the like kind, which had confined him to his room three weeks. I was defired to vifit her the 21ft of *July*, 1772; her pulfe was frequent and fomewhat full, her tongue foul, and thirft immoderate; fhe complained of head-ach, which had continued violent from the beginning, and prevented her having reft. Being ill near a week before I faw her, fome medi-

cines

cines had been given, and a blister applied : As I was informed there were signs of intermission towards morning, I directed the following draught :

℞.

> *Sal. Absinth.* Ɣ *i*
> *Succ. Limon.* ℥ *fs misce & affund.*
> *Decoct. Peruv. Cort.* ℥ *i*
> *Aq. Cinn. simp.* ℥ *iij fiat haustus 4ta quaq. hora exhibendus.*

Her complaints continued without much alteration the two following days ; but on the twenty-fourth her pulse was hard, the hands tremulous, and her eyes appeared bright and inflamed ; she was delirious by turns, and raved much in the night, which she passed without sleep. Eight ounces of blood were taken from the arm, and an emollient clyster was administered ; she afterwards took one of the following powders, which was ordered to be repeated in three hours, if the first produced no sensible effects.

℞. *Tart.*

℞.

Tart. emet. gr. ij
Magnes. alb. ʒ ſs contere & fiat Pulv. in ſex partes dividend.

The 25th, the febrile ſymptoms ſeemed to abate, and ſhe was ſomething better, having had refreſhing ſleep ſoon after bleeding, the preceding day : The powder firſt given proved gently emetic, and afterwards produced moiſture on the ſkin ; her pulſe being ſofter ; the draught, which was firſt preſcribed, was again repeated every four or five hours.

On the 27th, ſhe was ſtill more cool and free from fever, but extremely weak and languid ; and as the urine depoſited copious ſediment, I preſcribed the following draught, and deſired that weak broth, and light nouriſhment might be given as often as her ſtomach would bear.

B b 3   ℞. *Infus*

℞.

    Infus. Peruv. Cort. Fortiss. Confect. ℥ *iss*

    Extract. ejusd, moll, Ɵ *i*

    Spt. Lavend. c. ʒj

 Confect. Alkerm, ʒ *i fiat baustus 4ta quaq. hora exbibendus.*

She continued this medicine upwards of a week, and gradually gaining strength every day, at last perfectly recovered without *abortion.*

A preternatural intestinal discharge is usually called *Diarrhœa,* but when mixed with blood, or attended with pain and fever, it is then termed a DYSENTERY or BLOODY FLUX; This disease may arise from obstructed perspiration, corrupted food, or strong, drastic purgatives; it may also be communicated by infection, or brought on by sharp humors, which vellicate the interior

rior surface of the inteſtines, and determine the blood in too large a quantity to their tender veſſels.

There have been ſome few inſtances where blood was obſerved to proceed from the inteſtines, without any pain or loſs of ſtrength; and where the ſuppreſſion of this flux produced very dangerous ſymptoms, viz. vertigo, epilepſy, or even madneſs. It may therefore be reaſonably ſuppoſed, that ſuch evacuations were truly *critical*, and ſupplied the want of ſome other diſcharge; as that of bleeding piles, or perhaps the redundant blood, which is ſometimes carried off by the vagina, in the firſt months of pregnancy. Where the ſtools are ſanious and fœtid, attended with pain, fever, and teneſmus; it would be equally improper to put an early ſtop to the diſcharge.

It is not difficult to diſtinguiſh between the hæmorrhoidal flux, and dyſenteric blood; as the firſt is generally evacuated with inconſiderable pain, which is local and

Bb 4

confined to the rectum ; whereas, in dyfentery, the pain is often very acute and univerfal : Befides, in the hæmorrhoids ; the blood
is voided firſt, but in the other difeafe, it is
either mixed with fœces, or comes away
afterwards by the efforts of ſtraining.

When pain in the bowels is violent and
excruciating, but not foon followed by ſtools,
it may always be looked upon as a very *dangerous ſign*, which fhews that the fmall inteſtines are affected ; and if the patient is not
foon relieved, or particularly, if a difficulty
of fwallowing and hiccough come on ; it
denotes a *mortification*, and fhews that death
is at hand.

If the difeafe is long protracted, the inteſtines lofe their retentive and abforbent
power ; and the food taken into the ſtomach
inſtead of being converted into chyle, for
the nourifhment of the body, is hurried
thro' the inflamed inteſtines ; which being
ſtripped of their mucus and excoriated, are
affected with pain and *tormina*, from the

acrimony

acrimony of their contents : Hence, as the blood is deprived of attemperating fluids, the secretion of *urine and perspiration* becomes defective, and the patient will be nearly in the same situation as one after long fasting; consequently, from the rancid acrimony prevailing in the body, this disease, towards its conclusion, like most others, will become of the putrid kind.

In this disordered state of the female habit, the *fœtus in utero* being robbed of its nourishment will die ; and the *placentary vessels*, which from thence derive their energy and absorbing power, will now separate from the womb, like blighted fruit in vegetables, and the patient will miscarry.

Although the cause of this disease is different ; the treatment of it is so similar to that of the obstinate diarrhœa attending *Child-Bed Fever*, that I shall not trouble the reader with a repetition of what is laid down on that subject; but only observe, in those cases where, from the patient's excessive ceffive pain, one might have been tempted to direct *opiates*, they have feldom procured lafting eafe ; efpecially in the early ftate of this diforder ; but on the contrary, often increafe the oppreffion at ftomach and pain in the bowels, by leffening their expulfive motion, and locking up thofe corrupted, offending humors which ought to be carried off.   Therefore, *laxative medicines* which pafs without much irritation, with ricewater for common drink, and the frequent ufe of emollient clyfters, or thofe made with ftarch, where the mucus of the inteftines is abraded, will generally be found to afford relief.

Where the habit is plethoric, and much pain or fever attend ; the cure fhould commence with the lofs of blood, otherwife, it will not be abfolutely neceffary. Gentle emetics, fuch as the following, may then be given two or three times ; by intervals of three or four days, as the ftrength will permit :

℞. *Tart.*

℞.

   Tart. emet. gr. v.

   Magnef. alb. ʒ ſs

   Aq. Alex. fimp. ʒ vi

Oxymel. Scillet. ʒ ſs fiat miſtura cujus ſumat Cochlearia duo, oblata occaſione.

When the above medicine does not act as an emetic, it generally proves gently cathartic, or opens the cutaneous pores, which will be found greatly to affift in the cure, the fympathy between the ſkin and bowels being very remarkable; as may be obſerved in confumptive habits; for the habitual diarrhœa which then often attends is almoſt conſtantly better or worſe, as the colliquative ſweats are more or leſs profuſe. During the intervals, either of the following medicines may be given twice a-day, or oftener, according to the nature of the ſymptoms, or violence of the difcharge; and if the patient is much harraſſed with pain, and can get no reſt; thirty or forty drops of *thebaic tincture* may be occafionally added to the clyſter:

                      ℞. *Pulv.*

℞.

    Pulv. Rhei. gr. v.

    Confect. cardiac. Ә i fiat Bolus

℞.

    Pulv. Gall. Alep.

    ------ *Nucis Moschat. aa Ә fs*

    Syr. e Mecon. q. f. ut fiat Bolus.

When this disease is not attended with pain or fever, it then often arises from weakness and relaxation of the bowels ; and therefore, opiates and mild aftringents may be directed : The following bolus, or something of the like kind may be given twice a-day, with a tea-cup full of *aq. calcis,* to which, milk may be added in the quantity of a third part. A flannel shift should also be worn next the skin, and the feet kept extremely warm.

℞.

    Pulv. e Succin. c. gr. x.

    Confect. cardiac. Ә i fiat Bolus.

A lady in *Great Queen Street,* near twenty one years of age, and of a very delicate habit
of

of body ; in the feventh month of pregnancy, was affected with a diarrhœa, from
anxiety of mind. Though fhe took opiates
and other medicines, it continued almoft
without intermiffion, 'till the middle of the
eighth month ; whenthe pain in her bowels
became very violent, and blood with mucus
was difcharged with the ftools : She was
oppreffed with great ficknefs at ftomach,
and often threw up large quantities of ropy
yellow phlegm, mixed with blood. She
had very little appetite, or natural reft ;
complained much of head-ach, and labored
under a flow fever, and hectic heats, after
taking the leaft nourifhment : Her pulfe was
very languid and unequal ; in fhort, fhe
was reduced to the laft degree of weaknefs.

Opiates, which I at firft directed, fcarcely
procured her any fleep or lafting eafe,
neither was the diarrhœa abated ; being
conftantly difturbed feven or eight times
in the night, and during the twenty-four
hours, had fometimes fixteen or eighteen
motions,

motions, though at laſt, nothing was voided but a red, glairy ſubſtance, like flakes of half-putrified fleſh.   I then preſcribed the following powders, one of which, ſhe took in rice-water twice a-day.   The firſt pow-der made her ſick, but did not prove emetic, and although they always checked the looſeneſs, it never totally went off till within a few days after delivery ; at which time ſhe was better in all reſpects, and free from pain :

℞.

  Tart. emet. gr. ij

  Pulv. Contrayer. c. ℥ *i ſedule contere & fiat pulvis in ſex partes dividendus,*

Starch clyſters were adminiſtered, and her common drink was rice-water, with addition of gum arabic, which agreed with her better than any thing elſe.

After delivery, the purging commenced with as much violence as ever, attended with excruciating pain in her bowels ; the ſtools being very fœtid, and mixed with

           blood

blood as before. The next day, her pain was still exceffive, and the purging continued: Her nails began to turn black; fhe was feized with a fhivering fit, and immediately fell into *convulfions*, which lafted upwards of an hour; her body being agitated at different times with great violence. As the fit went off, and fhe feemed better, I was not fent for till the eighth day, at which time the purging returned, and the acute pain in her bowels threw her into another fit, which for a time, deprived her of all fenfe. *October* the 17th, 1772, I directed ftarch clyfters, with twenty drops of tinct. thebaic. to be given twice a-day, but in fmall quantities and only milk warm; her body and limbs were wrapped in warm flannels, and as I obferved that nothing relieved her fo much as the powders fhe had before taken, they were again repeated: She was better after the fecond powder; both the pain and diarrhœa being fenfibly abated. To avoid the danger

ger of relapfe, the powders were continued once or twice a-day for upwards of a week, and with care and proper nourifhment, fhe gradually recovered. Towards the end of the month, fhe took the following draught night and morning for ten days :

   ℞.

     Cort. peruv. Pulv. ℥ *fs*
     Fol. Rofar. rub. ficc.
     Cort. Cinn. aa ʒ *i*
     Aq. bullient. ℥ *x poft macerat. idon. cola.*
   ℞.

     Hujus colat. ℥ *ifs*
     Tinct. Japonic. ʒ *ii*
     Confect. Alkerm. ʒ *i fiat hauftus nocteq.*
mane exhibendus.

  This medicine affifted her greatly, by ftrengthening the bowels and increafing her appetite, and at laft fhe was reftored to her former ftate of health ; but from taking cold, or other accidental caufes, is ftill apt to be flightly affected with her former complaints.

                          The

THE late illustrious *Baron Van Swieten*, in the fifth and last volume of his *Commentaries*, a work which will render his name venerable to posterity, remarks the following circumstances, from his own experience, in what relates to the *Small-Pox*, viz. that the method of preparation usually observed, before the artificial communication of that disease, may be omitted without danger : for at the *Orphan-house*, situated in the suburbs of *Vienna* ; though there was not any variation in the diet of those *inoculated*, from the rest ; no inconvenience was perceived to follow. But it is to be observed, that they all breathed the open air for the whole day, and slept in spacious and lofty bedchambers, well perflated ; hence arose the opinion which now prevails with some ; that those who labor under the *natural small-pox* will recover as easily as others who are *inoculated* ; without much regard to diet or medicine, provided that they sufficiently enjoy the influence of *fresh air*.

C c   According

According to the calculation of Dr. *Jurin*, several years ago, about one in fix died by the natural fmall pox ; but of thofe who were inoculated fcarcely one in forty-eight. If the calculation is juft, it appears that this deftructive malady is rendered much milder by the method of treatment ; fince the number of thofe who die, compared to thofe who recover, is happily now very fmall ; even in the natural fort, except they happen to *women with child* ; or during an unhealthy feafon of the year, where they become complicated with other *difeafes of the epidemic kind* : This favorable circumftance, feems principally owing to the fame treatment in the natural fmall pox, as had been found fo remarkably beneficial in thofe communicated by inoculation, in which, fcarcely *one in four hundred* now die.

Abftemious, laxative diet, will be proper in the beginning ; fuch as that of roafted apples, ripe oranges, or other cooling vegetables

tables of the solutive kind ; also milk-pottage, or gruel sweetened with honey.

In adults and those of strong habits, bleeding is generally necessary, being so far from retarding the eruption, that it appears more kindly after that evacuation. One of the following powders will then be proper, and may be given for two or three nights successively, as occasion requires :

℞

Calomel. ppt.

Sulph. præcipitat. aa gr. x

Tart. emetic gr. ij contere & fiat pulv. subtiliss. in sex partes dividend.

As soon as the eruption appears ; if the inflammatory symptoms run high, and it seems to rush out too hastily ; the following cathartic draught should immediately be given ; especially, if the previous use of the powders has not sufficiently emptied the bowels :

Infus.

R.

Infus. Sen. limoniat. ℥ ij
Mann. calab. ℥ iij *solv.*
Spt. Lavend. c. ℥ i *fiat hauftus.*

During the fymptoms of *eruptive fever,* the patient may drink as much *cold fpring water* as her thirft requires. At this time fhe ought, by no means, to be confined to her bed, or a warm room, but fhould *walk* gently about in the frefh, open air, taking care at her return, not to expofe herfelf to it in a full ftream, by fitting between open doors or windows; and however ftrange the practice might at firft appear, it is now fufficiently juftified and confirmed by the conftant and daily fuccefs which attends it.

This method was firft followed and re-commended by *Sydenham,* who was often unmercifully cenfured for venturing to de-part from the common practice; but being convinced by repeated experience of its fa-lutary effect, and aiming at nothing fo much as the public good, he fubmitted to

undeferved

undeferved reproaches, and thought himfelf amply repaid by the fatisfaction arifing from a confcientious difcharge of his duty, and the benevolent feelings of his own heart. But although the fuccefs attending the prefent practice, is chiefly and originally owing to the fagacious and incomparable *Sydenham*; furely, thofe who have fince been the means of boldly oppofing popular errors, and permanently eftablifhing that method which contributes to the prefervation of thoufands, alfo deferve their proper fhare of praife.

By the liberal ufe of cold water, and the influence of *frefh air*, the fick find themfelves revived in a moft extraordinary manner; the frequency and fulnefs of the pulfe is obferved to abate, thirft grows lefs, and the fymptomatic fever being almoft extinguifhed, a free perfpiration ufually fucceeds, accompanied with a favorable eruption; after which, nothing more feems neceffary, but only to forward the maturation of the puftules, by fupplying the patient

C c 3   plentifully

plentifully with milk and water, tea, or any thing of the like kind. At this time, the body ought to be kept cool and temperate by emollient clyfters and gentle laxatives, as the ftate of the bowels may require.

Where the variolous eruption is complicated with a thick *milliary rafh*, it will be proper to leffen the cooling regimen, and allow the patient white-wine whey, or weak broth, inftead of cold fluids.

A *phrenzy* happening the third or fourth day after the eruption, is an alarming fymptom. *Bleeding* and emollient clyfters may here be directed, and the patient fhould be kept cool ; *leeches* may be applied to her temples, and the following julep taken occafionally ; alfo barley water, with the addition of nitre, and vegetable acids for common drink.

R.

Aq. font. purifs. ℨ vij
Spt. nitri dulc. ℨ iij
Syr. Violar. ℨ fs fiat Julepum.

Purples

Purples on the fkin denote great danger, efpecially if the pock is confluent ; but where *bloody urine* is voided at the fame time, it may be looked upon as a mortal fign. Thofe appearances, however, are not always the genuine fymptoms of the difeafe, but often arife from heating regimen, and too great a degree of the circulating power. As the firft may be owing to a putrid diffolution of blood, they are much more dangerous than the other, and therefore, a diftinction fhould be made refpecting their treatment. In thofe of the *putrid kind*, antifeptic medicines may be given ; as a decoction of *bark*, with *elixir of vitriol*, or tincture of rofes ; but in the *inflammatory fort*, bleeding and laxatives with nitrous drinks may be directed.

Towards the height, about the eighth or ninth day, the fecondary, putrid fever, which might otherwife then commence, is to be prevented by *purgatives*, if poffible ; therefore the fame cathartic draught which

C c 4

was

was given in the beginning, may be repeated every other day, or as the strength will permit. *Opiates* are now proper, especially after the operation of the purge, or when the patient is reftlefs and in pain; but fhould a dilirium or difficulty of breathing come on, they fhould be wholly omitted.

Where the circulation flags, and *the* puftules, inftead of maturating and growing fuller, feem to flatten and look pale; *fnake-root, faffron,* and fuch like warm medicines, have been recommended; but as far as I have been able to obferve, nothing has equalled the good effects of *James's powder,* or *emetic tartar,* given at firft in fuch quantity as to prove gently emetic, and afterwards, to act as an alterative only.

Some direct the limbs to be bliftered at this time, and others do not fcruple to give *cold water*; and indeed, confidering its falutary effects in the beginning, fuch a ftep does

not

not appear altogether exceptionable ; particularly if it be earneftly defired by the patient.

Where the *falivation*, which ufually attends the confluent fmall-pox, fuddenly ftops, the patient generally dies about the eleventh or twelfth day ; efpecially, if her face and hands do not then begin to fwell, or where fome other evacuation does not immediately follow. To encourage the fpitting, the head may be held over the fteam of warm water, and the following *gargarifm* may frequently be ufed :

℞

 Aq. hordeat. ℥j
 Sal. Ammon. crud. ℥ ij
 Mell. ℥ fs *fiat Gargarifma.*

Thofe who are feized with *fmall-pox* in the pregnant ftate, have generally much more eafy and expeditious labors than other women : However extraordinary this circumftance may appear, I have feen it verified in many inftances ; and indeed, never

yet

yet found it otherwife in any cafe, where the labor was ftrictly natural. It cannot be owing to the general weaknefs and relaxation of the body; in confequence of which the child might be fuppofed to meet with lefs refiftance in the birth; for if fo, the *uterus* would participate of the effect, and its expulfive force being diminifhed, labor, inftead of being fooner over, would probably be rendered more tedious and lingering.

In the *mifcellan. natur. curios.* may be found feveral inftances of women dying gravid, who were afterwards delivered of living children; *Horftius* alfo relates a hiftory of this kind; and *Raymond,* in his book *de ortu infantum coutra naturam,* is full of fuch wonderful ftories; which are fitter to entertain old women and nurfes, than rational men, yet the celebrated *Hoffman,* who does not feem behind hand with any of them in credulity, attempts ferioufly to account for fuch extraordinary births, by the expanfion of putrid air, in the body of the foetus.

Several

Several years ago, I was sent for to a tradesman's wife in *Mount-street, Berkley-square*, who was taken with labor just at the height of the *small-pox*; but being then at some distance, she was delivered without any assistance, before I got there, and died the next day.

July the 12th 1767, *Ann Moody* was admitted into the *Westminster Lying-In Hospital*, with symptoms of labor, and being otherwise very ill, was allowed to remain longer than usual before delivery. The *small-pox* appeared soon after admission, but as the eruption was at first taken for a rash, I was not acquainted with it until several days after: She was delivered of a dead child, about eight months old; the ninth day after the eruption, without much pain, or the usual efforts of labor: The pustules were of the confluent kind, and very thick on her skin, together with *purples*, for which a *decoction of bark* with *elixir of vitriol*

was

was given, but without effect; for she died delirious the day after delivery.

January the 14th, 1768, *Esther Grace* was admitted into the *Hospital*, and delivered the third day after, of a living child, and at her full time : Though her pains were very inconsiderable, the birth was so quick and easy as not to require any kind of assistance : The next day the *small-pox* appeared. She was carefully removed in a chair the fifth day, and died three days after, being the eighth from the time of eruption. The child was nursed and taken care of in the Hospital, but died at eight days old ; though without any eruption on its body, or other symptoms of small-pox.

February the 8th, 1770, I attended Mrs. C——n, at *Lambeth*, who had the *small-pox* in the fifth month of pregnancy : She was young, and of a strong, healthy constitution, but very full of eruption, which was rather of the confluent than distinct kind. As I was called to her in the beginning of the disease,

difeafe, it was treated by the cooling regimen
already mentioned ; the weather being at
the fame time intenfely cold. The *fpitting*,
which had affifted her greatly, began to diminifh very much, a little after the height.
About the twelfth or thirteenth day, fhe
was excceeding ill ; the fymptoms of the fecondary fever were then violent, and fhe
was unable to fpeak or fwallow, except with
great difficulty. Nothing at this time relieved fo much as a *purging draught*, which
fhe took every other day : As her ftrength
and fpirits were always better, and the bad
fymptoms evidently lefs violent on the days
fhe took the purge, I directed it to be made
weaker, and repeated it for three days fuc-
ceffively. She now recovered daily, and at
the end of three weeks, was able to take the
air ; but what appeared rather extraordinary, although fhe had efcaped abortion during
the difeafe, fhe mifcarried about a month
after her firft going abroad.

About

About the fame time, viz. *February* the 24th, 1770, I was defired to vifit Mrs. *P————r*, near the *Hofpital*, who then labored under the fmall pox, in the eighth month of pregnancy. Her mid-wife informed me fhe was delivered foon after the eruption appeared, with fo much precipitation, that the infant fell on the floor, as fhe was affifted in getting off the clofe-ftool. I faw her the ninth day from the eruption, which was large in quantity and of the worft confluent kind : *Broad purple fpots* almoft every where over-fpread that part of her fkin where the puf-tules were wanting ; there were befides, fe-veral fmall veficles on her breaft filled with a yellowifh fluid, like the ferum of blood, and fome with *bloody ichor* ; but as her water came away involuntarily, I could not tell whether the urine was bloody or not. She was alfo delirious : Indeed, I never faw the difeafe attended with more malignant fymp-toms ; and though there were no hopes of

her

her recovery, I directed the following draught, and desired that the fluids she was able to swallow might be acidulated with lemon-juice ;

℞

  Decoct. Cort, Peruv. ℥ *iss*
  Extract. ejusd. moll. ℈ *i*
  Elix. Vitriol. acid. g^{tt}. xxx
  Tinct. Cort. Peruv. ʒ *iij*
  Confect. Alkerm. ʒ *i fiat haustus alternis*
horis exhibendus.

She died the next day about twelve o'clock, being the tenth from the first appearance of the eruption.

October the 21ſt, 1772, *Elizabeth Lee* was delivered in the *Weſtminſter Lying-in Hoſpital* of a living child, in the eighth month of pregnancy : As the *ſmall-pox* appeared on her ſkin next day, ſhe was carefully removed to her own apartment by her friends, where ſhe recovered ; the diſeaſe being mild, and the eruption of the diſtinct kind. The child was ſeized with it a fortnight after ;

            but

but I had no opportunity to inform myfelf whether it lived or not.

Notwithftanding I never faw any inftance where infants were born with *variolous eruption*, 'till the following cafe mentioned by Mr. *Waftall* occurred ; yet examples may be found in the *Philofophical Tranfactions, Bartholin's Medical Epiftles, &c.* where the body of the new-born infant has been found overfpread with puftules ; which, confidering the intercourfe between the mother and it, during geftation, is not to be wondered at.

Account of a Woman who had the Small-Pox during Pregnancy, and who feemed to have communicated that Difeafe to the Fœtus. By John Hunter, *Efq. F. R. S. from* Mr. Wastall's *Letter on the fame fubject.*

December 30, 1776, I was fent for to Mrs. Ford, a healthy woman, about twenty-two years of age, who was pregnant with her firft child. She had come out of the country about three months before. Soon after her arrival in town fhe was feized with

the

the small pox, and had been under the care of Messieurs HAWKINS and GRANT, who have favoured me with the particulars here annexed.

I called upon her in the afternoon; she complained of violent gripings in her bowels, darting down to the *pubes*. On examining I found the *os tincæ* a little dilated, with other symptoms of approaching labour. I sent her an anodyne, spermaceti emulsion, and desired to be called, if her pains increased. I was sent for. The labour advanced very slowly; her pains were lasting and severe; she was delivered of a dead child, with some difficulty.

Observing an eruption all over the body of the child, and several of the *pustules* filled with matter, I examined them more particularly; and recollecting that Dr. LEAKE, in his Introductory Lecture to the Practice of Midwifery, had observed that it might be necessary to inquire, whether those adults who are said totally to escape the small pox,

D d

have

have not been previously affected with it in the womb; I sent a note to Dr. LEAKE, and likewise to Dr. HUNTER, in hopes of ascertaining a fact hitherto much doubted. Dr. LEAKE came the same evning, and saw the child. Dr. HUNTER came afterwards, with Mr. CRUICKSHANKS, and examined it; also Mr. JOHN HUNTER and Mr. FALCONER; who all concurred with me, that the eruption on the child was the small pox. Dr. HUNTER thought the eruption so like the small pox, that he could hardly doubt; but said, that in all other cases of the same kind, he had met with, the child *in utero* escaped the contagion.

It appears, from Mr. *Grant's* Notes, that the eruption appeared on Mrs. *Ford*, in the evening of the 8th December, and that she was delivered the 31st, that is, twenty-three days after the appearance of the eruption.

A Cafe no lefs *curious* and *extraordinary*, I received from my *Pupil* Mr. *Head*, as follows:

To Dr. LEAKE.

London. Nov. 30, 1778.

SIR,

I fome time fince mentioned to you a cafe of *Inoculation* for the fmall pox, which you thought fingular. The hiftory of it you have below, and may depend upon the facts, as the patient was my own.

I am, Sir,

With the greateft refpect,

Your moft obedient fervant,

ISAAC HEAD.

In the beginning of September, 1766, I was defired to inoculate a boy of five years old, for the fmall pox; the parents at the fame time informing me they wifhed it fhould be performed in about a fortnight.

I had often thought it poffible, that the variolous matter might be capable of raifing an inflammation in the arm of a perfon who

D d 2   had

had paſſed the ſmall pox, and that if it came to any degree of ſuppuration, might probably retain ſo much of the nature of ſmall pox, as to infect a perſon who never had the diſorder, by inoculating in the uſual manner.

To try this experiment, I inoculated myſelf in the arm. I was much pleaſed to find an inflammation come regularly on in as ſhort a ſpace of time, and with as much violence, as I had ever ſeen in thoſe who never paſſed the ſmall pox.

On the evening of the 6th day I ſuddenly felt the ſame kind of ſenſation, as if a ſpark of fire had got on the part. On examination, I found it prodigiouſly inflamed ; there was a veſication about the ſize of a ſmall pea, and redneſs extended round it, under the cuticle, to the ſize of a ſixpence. On the ninth day it was full of pus, and the circle extended to the ſize of a crown. On the tenth day I inoculated the child from this puſtule, in the common way.

I

I have the pleasure to assure you, that this child had the small pox in as regular a manner, and with the usual concomitant symptoms, as any I ever had under my care. He was very sick for a day before the pustules made their appearance, and had a great many of them. I inoculated *seven other children from this patient, and none of them failed having the small pox.*

One of those was so ill, that I was very apprehensive he would have died, but fortunately he also recovered.   I. HEAD.

An uncommon case is related by *Van Swieten,* as it happened under the observation of Dr. *Watson* in *London,* viz. a woman who had been for some time pregnant, and who long before had the *small-pox,* was very assiduous in attending her servant maid, who then laboured under that disease : In due time, she was happily delivered, and brought forth a healthy female child, where *evident marks of its having had the eruption, appeared on the skin.* When this child's brother was

inoculated

inoculated four years after, Dr. *Watson* had leave from the parents, to inoculate her likewife; but the operation was attended with very different effects in thofe different fubjects; for the puftules appeared in the boy, who foon happily recovered from the difeafe; but the girl after drooping two days, became very well again, and remained totally free from the eruption.

A cafe fomething fimilar to this is alfo mentioned by Dr. *Mead* in treating of the fmall pox. He fuppofes that where the child is born before the perfect maturation of the puftules in the mother, it will then more probably efcape the difeafe; and that the danger arifing to women at this time, who fuffer abortion, will be in proportion to the lofs of blood, after the feparation of the *placenta* from the uterus: But there is not fufficient reafon to adopt this laft opinion; for even what Dr. *Mead* himfelf afterwards afferts does not correfpond with it, viz. that the fmall pox have generally been found

found moſt mild, when they ſucceed ſome
conſiderable evacuation, whether natural or
artificial.

Van Swieten informs us, that the celebrated *Boerhaave* attended a lady in the ſixth
month of pregnancy, who labored under
the worſt kind of *confluent ſmall pox* : notwithſtanding which, ſhe proceeded to the
full period of her time, and was then delivered of a healthy male child, which had
not the leaſt veſtige or appearance of the
diſeaſe.

From the above extraordinary circumſtance, which was probably owing to the peculiar ſtructure of the *placenta* and its power to abſorb from the womb ſuch juices
only as were ſalutary and nutritious ; even
when the whole maſs of the mother's blood
was tainted with *variolous infection* ; one
would incline to think, that *hereditary
diſeaſes* are providentially leſs frequent than
they otherwiſe would have been, and
that the perfection of animal fluid
depends

depends more upon the fecreting organ, than the general mafs from which they are ftrained off. This property, with which the placenta feems endowed, is beautifully illuftrated, by what may be feen in *vegetables*; where two plants of different qualities both draw their nourifhment from the fame earth; the one a *deadly poifon*, the other friendly to the human fyftem, or perhaps an *antidote* to the former; and this is ftill further exemplified in grafting branches of one tree into the ftem of another; for the juices of the laft, will from thence be fo far divefted of their natural qualities, by paffing thro' different ftrainers, as only to produce the fame kind of fruit, with that of the tree, from which fuch branches were taken,

THE END.

POSTSCRIPT.

The following Gentlemen, befides many others, who either went abroad, or fettled in different parts of the kingdom, which I cannot recollect, attended my LECTURES, at the times already mentioned; moft of whom took *notes*, and therefore, to fuch I refer for a confirmation of the facts mentioned in the *Introduction* to the preceding obfervations.

MR. C. M. Thode, Surgeon to the Emprefs of *Ruffia, Peterfburgh.*

Mr. Crowder, *Leadenhall-ftreet, London.*

Mr. John Blake, *Briftol.*

Mr. William Slater, Houfe Apothecary to the Difpenfary, for the relief of the Poor, *Alderfgate-ftreet, London.*

Mr. Richard Newland, *Chichefter, Suffex.*

Mr. Edward Yale, *Catharine-ftreet, London.*

Mr.

POSTSCRIPT.

Mr. Robert Hobſon, *Bernard-Caſtle,* county of *Durham.*

Mr. Charles Lightfoot, *Whitby, Yorkſhire.*

Mr. William Cartwright, *Wenleck, Salop.*

Mr. Joſeph Dawſon, *Eaſt-Indies.*

Mr. Thomas Tubb, *Lambourn, Berkſhire.*

Mr. Thomas Parkinſon, *Kirkham, Lancaſhire.*

Mr. William Harffy, *Caſtle-ſtreet, Leiceſter-fields.*

Mr. William Sexton, *Thame, Oxfordſhire.*

Mr. John Cauſer, Houſe Surgeon to St. *George's Hoſpital,* 1771.

Mr. Robert Pope, *Staines, Middleſex.*

Mr. Lewis Poignand, *Duke-ſtreet, Weſtminſter.*

Mr. Thomas Hammond, *Little Newport-ſtreet, Newport Market.*

Mr. Jeremiah Wilkinſon, *Scarborough.*

Mr. John Marſh, *Half-Moon-ſtreet, Piccadilly.*

Mr. J. Rackham, *Bungay, Suffolk.*

Mr. Thomas Inman, *St. Oſyth, Eſſex.*

Mr. Edward Weeks, *Weſtfield, Suſſex.*

Mr.

P O S T S C R I P T.

Mr. H. Dickinson, *Cecil-street. Strand.*

Mr. Edward Ford, *Bristol.*

Mr. James Bromley, *Rochester, Kent.*

Mr. P. Weaver, *Hermitage, Tower-Hill.*

Mr. D. Raven, *Hatfield Peveral, Essex.*

Mr. Thomas Bredall, *Mattocks-street, London.*

Mr. J. Dutton, *Manchester.*

Mr. Thomas Brittain, *Rugley, Staffordshire.*

Mr. Thomas Parker, *Gloucester.*

Mr. Thomas Owen, *Rye, Sussex.*

Mr. James Scaife, *Carlisle, Cumberland.*

Mr. William Younge, *Shiffnall, Shropshire.*

Mr. James Bumpstead, *Castle Heddington, Essex.*

Mr. William Young, *Georgia, America.*

Mr. ——— Druitt, *Winburn, Dorsetshire.*

Mr. Thomas Shute, *Bristol.*

Mr. James Travers, *Military Hospital, Granada.*

Dr. William Moore, *Brook-street.*

Mr. Thomas Vigur's, *Leostoffe, Suffolk.*

Mr. Henry Bickersteth, *Kirbylonsdale, Westmoreland.*

Mr.

POSTSCRIPT.

Mr. Edward Horler, *Tooting, Surry.*

Mr. ———— Wilson, jun. *Henrietta-street, Covent Garden.*

Mr. Charles Chafmore, *Epfom, Surry.*

Mr. Robert Turner, *Enfield.*

Mr. John Manning, ⎫
Mr. Jofeph Lord, ⎭ *Bofton, New-England.*

INDEX

INDEX.

A

INDEX.

I N D E X.

INDEX.

Child—

INDEX.

E e

INDEX.

INDEX.

Fluids,

INDEX.

I N D E X.

INDEX.

L

M

INDEX.

INDEX.

INDEX.

S. SPECU-

INDEX.

S.

Styptics

INDEX.

I N D E X.

F I N I S.